Discipler's Guide
Encouraging the Growing Believer

Billie Hanks, Jr.

 INTERNATIONAL EVANGELISM ASSOCIATION
SALADO, TEXAS 76571

 WORD MINISTRY RESOURCES
WACO, TX 76702

For more information about this ministry, write or call:

INTERNATIONAL EVANGELISM ASSOCIATION
PO BOX 1174
SALADO, TEXAS 76571-1174
(817) 947-3030

Printed in the United States of America

Scripture quotations identified NASB are from *The New American Standard Bible*, copyright © 1960, 1962, 1971, 1972, 1973, 1975, by the Lockman Foundation and used by permission. Unless otherwise indicated, Scripture quotations on pages 1-116 are from *The New American Standard Bible*.

Scripture quotations identified NIV are from *The Holy Bible: New International Version,* © 1978 by the New York International Bible Society. Used by permission of Zondervan Bible Publishers. Unless otherwise indicated, Scripture quotations on pages 117-207 are from *The Holy Bible: New International Version*.

Scripture quotations identified KJV are from *The Holy Bible: King James Version*.

Scripture quotations identified NKJV are from *The New King James Bible,* © 1979 Thomas Nelson, Inc., Publishers.

Scripture quotations identified LB are from *The Living Bible Paraphrased*, (Wheaton: Tyndale House Publishers, © 1971).

Scripture quotations identified MLB are from *The Modern Language Bible*, (The Berkeley Version in Modern English), copyright © 1959 by Zondervan Publishing House.

Scripture quotations identified PH are from *The New Testament in Modern English,* copyright © 1958, 1960, 1972 by J.B. Phillips.

Scripture quotations identified as JB are from *The Jerusalem Bible,* copyright © 1966, 1967, and 1968 by Darton, Longman & Todd Ltd. and Doubleday & Company, Inc.

This book is
dedicated
to those who love
the harvest.

CONTENTS

ACKNOWLEDGMENTS

For International Evangelism's staff, this new edition of *A Call To Joy* represents a milestone in our positive experience with follow-up. We would like to thank you and every other Discipler for giving life to these materials by prayerfully teaching them to a new or growing Christian.

My personal thanks go to Rev. Sam Cook, Dr. Herbert Shipp, and our other former staff members for their original contributions toward this effort. In addition, I would like to thank Mr. Randy Craig for his conceptual and editing skills, Rev. Dan Nelson for his creative and artistic gifts, and Mr. Randy Ray for his faithful support in typesetting and design. They have truly made this new edition a labor of love and dedication to Christ.

The literary skills and disciple-making experience of Robert Coleman, LeRoy Eims, Gary Kuhne, and Gene Warr offer invaluable insight and inspiration to this basic New Testament emphasis on follow-up and discipleship.

My prayer is that each person who uses *A Call To Joy* will experience the great satisfaction that comes from feeding the Lord's lambs and sheep!

Yours in that joy,

Billie Hanks, Jr.

DISCIPLER'S GUIDE INTRODUCTION

USING *A CALL TO JOY*:

This book is designed to enable you to personally follow-up new believers and new members as they enter the fellowship of your church. The assimilation process is accomplished by forming a Christ-centered friendship with each new member. During these relationships, you will encourage them to establish basic spiritual disciplines that will lead toward consistent spiritual growth.

CONTENTS OF *A CALL TO JOY*:

Discipler's Packet	**Timothy's Packet**
Discipler's Guide	*Timothy's Guide*
Spiritual Journal	*Spiritual Journal*
Steps to Peace with God	*Steps to Peace with God*

EXPLANATION OF TERMS

Note: In this material, the Discipler (mentor) and the Timothy (apprentice) will be referred to as "he," "him," and "his." The generic use of these pronouns refer to both male and female.

A. **Discipler** – A Christian who is growing consistently in his relationship with Jesus Christ and is showing a younger believer how to *mature* in his faith and *share* his witness naturally.

   Paul said, *"Follow my example, as I follow the example of Christ."* (1 Corinthians 11:1, NIV)

B. **Timothy** – A believer who is seeking to grow spiritually by spending time with a more experienced Christian. This equipping process is derived from the New Testament example of Paul who *taught* and *trained* a growing young believer named Timothy.

   "And he came also to Derbe and to Lystra. And behold, a certain disciple was there, named Timothy, the son of a Jewish woman who was a believer, but his father was a Greek, and he was well spoken of by the brethren who were in Lystra and Iconium. Paul wanted this man to go with him; and he took him and circumcised him because of the Jews who were in those parts, for they all knew that his father was a Greek." (Acts 16:1-3)

   "And the things which you have heard from me in the presence of many witnesses, these entrust to faithful men, who will be able to teach others also." (2 Timothy 2:2)

   Note: For best results, we recommend that men disciple men and women disciple women.

C. **Session** – An inspirational time of 1¹/₂ to 2 hours during which a Timothy meets with his Discipler for Christian fellowship and spiritual instruction. *A Call To Joy* is normally completed in 7 to 10 weeks. The completion rate is solely based upon the individual needs of your Timothy, so do not rush. Enjoy each session together!

D. Weekly Spiritual Growth Assignments – Inspirational activities designed for both you and your Timothy to complete between the scheduled sessions. These assignments are printed after each session in your *Discipler's Guide* and in the *Timothy's Guide*. They focus on daily Quiet Times, personal prayer, weekly sermon note-taking, and inspirational reading. As a Discipler, you will need to complete *both* the Timothy's Assignment and Discipler's Assignment each week.

WHY *A CALL TO JOY?*

Jesus expressed his personal concern about follow-up and spiritual nurture when he said, *"Peter do you love Me? . . . Feed My lambs . . . Take care of My sheep . . . Feed My sheep."* (John 21:15-17, NIV) When you invest the time to follow-up new believers and members, it is actually an evidence of your deep love for Christ.

Increasingly, churches are realizing the importance of good follow-up and new member assimilation. Different methods are being used to accomplish this objective. Some churches offer Pastor's classes, fill-in-the-blank Bible studies, or special follow-up meetings.

Experience has demonstrated that these approaches, though desirable, are still inadequate when used alone. After years of field testing, we have concluded that the most effective method for new member assimilation is encouraging Christ-centered friendships. There are several reasons why this personal approach to follow-up has proven so successful:

Friendship Factor: Studies show that unless a new member establishes one or more meaningful relationships within a few months, he is likely to quietly leave through the "back door." *A Call To Joy's* follow-up process provides an environment for friendship and seeks to meet the immediate spiritual needs of each new member.

Encouragement: The New Testament pattern for spiritual growth is learning from the example of a more mature believer. Paul said,

"The things you have learned and received and heard and seen in me, practice these things; and the God of peace shall be with you." (Philippians 4:9)

Individual Care: New believers require special care and *A Call To Joy*'s friendship based follow-up process provides that opportunity naturally.

"But we proved to be gentle among you, as a nursing mother tenderly cares for her own children." (1 Thessalonians 2:7)

Flexible Schedule: If for any reason you or your Timothy are unavoidably detained from meeting together, you can simply re-schedule for another day. In this way, important material is never missed.

Freedom of Discussion: In a personal friendship there is an atmosphere of openness, so questions can be discussed honestly. In *A Call To Joy*, you and your Timothy can meet as many times as you desire.

Mutual Spiritual Growth: As you encourage new members, you will also be challenged to grow as *". . . iron sharpens iron . . ."* in your friendship. This process creates positive motivation for continued spiritual development! Our mandate is abundantly clear:

". . .Grow in the grace and knowledge of our Lord and Savior Jesus Christ. To Him be the glory, both now and to the day of eternity." (2 Peter 3:18)

MEETING WITH YOUR TIMOTHY

A. Your Coordinator will *call* and provide the needed follow-up information regarding your new Timothy. Space is provided to record this information on pages 211-214 of this *Discipler's Guide*.

B. Prayerfully attempt to contact your Timothy within *24 hours,* and schedule a time and place for your first meeting together.

Consider these possible meeting places:

1. **A restaurant**
2. **Their home**
3. **Your home**
4. **The church building**

C. Stop by the church building and collect a *Timothy Packet* for your new trainee.

D. Your Team Leader will *call* you at a mutually agreeable time each week. Be sure to let him know if you have completed the current session and if you have any new prayer needs.

E. Report your *victories* and any unusual *concerns* to your Coordinator or Team Leader. In the process, seek to provide personal help, but always be careful not to break your Timothy's confidence.

F. Seek to lead your Timothy as far as he/she is willing to go in their spiritual growth process!

PREPARING FOR EACH SESSION

Turn to page 1 of this *Discipler's Guide*. You will notice that some of the material is boxed and other parts are not. The boxed material appears *only* in your *Discipler's Guide* while the unboxed material appears in *both* the *Timothy's Guide* and *Discipler's Guide*. The boxes contain "teaching notes" (illustrations, amplifications, and questions) to be shared and discussed during each session.

You will teach from this *Discipler's Guide* during your times together. The unboxed material should be read aloud during each session. If your Timothy is comfortable reading aloud, you should ask him to join you in verbally reading this material. This involvement will help him feel like a participant, and it will give you additional time to think ahead for each discussion segment. When you arrive at a box in your *Discipler's Guide*, simply give the illustration or amplification. If indicated, ask the questions found in the boxes and use a "highlighter" to mark the key words. This will help "trigger" your thoughts for discussion.

You will notice that within each box, there are *shaded* sentences and *unshaded* sentences. Unshaded sentences mean that you will make a direct statement to your Timothy. Example: "Let's get right into our Bible study. Today we will focus on understanding the Gospel." Shaded sentences mean that you, the Discipler, are receiving a specific instruction to carry out. Example: Seek to determine your Timothy's relationship with Christ during this session.

Your *Discipler's Guide* expands each page of the *Timothy's Guide* into two pages. This enables you to have "teaching notes" to guide your discussions. This design allows your *Discipler's Guide* to have the same page numbers as the *Timothy's Guide*.

Some of the boxes contain blanks. Use these blanks for additional personal illustrations or amplifications which you wish to cover with your Timothy.

Notice that some of the material contained in boxes will have page numbers. Example: (See page 197, #1). When you see a page number, turn to Appendix A and simply find the corresponding number. Then read the detailed illustration or amplification. *You will want to study this material before each meeting so you can present it naturally without having to turn to the Appendix during your session.*

Important: Turn to page 8 in this *Discipler's Guide*. Notice that *your blanks* have already been completed, but the blanks in the *Timothy's Guide* have not. These blanks are designed to be filled in by your Timothy *during each session. They are not homework*, so he will never know these answers unless you tell him during your sessions together.

A. To anticipate your Timothy's questions, you should plan to stay at least two weeks *ahead* in these materials, and spend enough time in prayer to arrive at each session with a *prepared* heart and mind!

B. Your Timothy will sometimes have *questions*, and they will be important to him, so take the necessary time to answer each one.

If you do not know the answer, you can simply say, "I'm not sure, but I will try to find out and discuss it with you next week." Always be sure to remember his questions. Your pastor, Coordinator, or Bible teacher will serve as a resource person when you need their help.

C. Seek to be *consistent,* but always slow down if your Timothy has a personal need that requires extra prayer and time together. Remember that covering these sessions at the suggested rate of speed is not important. What ultimately matters is meeting your Timothy's spiritual needs.

D. Try to schedule your weekly meetings with the possibility of *flexible* endings, so you can both *relax* and enjoy your time together!

YOUR MINISTRY AS A DISCIPLER

A. As a Discipler, you will be demonstrating the path to personal growth by modeling the following spiritual disciplines:

1. **A Daily Quiet Time**.
2. **Daily Prayer**.
3. **Sermon Note-taking**.
4. **Scripture Memory**.
5. **Natural Lifestyle Evangelism**.

B. Since you will be training your Timothy by example, it will be important for you to demonstrate the value of using a *Spiritual Journal.*

C. Make sure that your Timothy has an up-to-date translation of the Bible. The NKJV and NIV are excellent versions for new believers. Wide margin Bibles are also helpful because they will allow him to record extended insights during personal Bible study. (See the Resource Section, page 113.)

D. During *A Call To Joy,* your primary objective will be to lay the foundation for your Timothy's long-term spiritual development. *A Call To Joy* teaches the daily Quiet Time as the primary means of personal spiritual growth. *A Call To Growth* (the next step after *A Call To Joy*) teaches independent Bible study, prayer and personal witness. Your task will be to assist your Timothy as he builds his *own convictions* about the valuable disciplines being taught. His personal convictions will give him the motivation required for spiritual growth. For this reason, the positive impact of this training will be with him long after your meetings have been completed.

E. Avoid merely asking your Timothy to *do* his assignments. Encourage him to personally discover the spiritual purpose behind each new step. Point out that *understanding,* coupled with *application,* produces spiritual vitality!

YOUR SPIRITUAL OBJECTIVES:

A. Help your Timothy develop a *long-term spiritual growth process* that will continue long after your meetings have concluded.

B. Lead your Timothy to establish strong *personal convictions* about the Lord Jesus Christ!

C. Provide your Timothy with a *Biblical foundation* for future spiritual development.

D. Encourage your Timothy to *share his faith* and *convictions* with others.

AS YOU BEGIN:

A. Express *excitement* about your Timothy's relationship with Christ!

B. Progress at a *rate* that is realistic and enjoyable.

C. Be *sensitive* to his personal needs, and look forward to informal times together.

D. Seek to foster a *team* spirit by emphasizing that you will *both* be growing spiritually as you meet together!

A CALL TO GROWTH

Experience has shown that a high percentage of those who begin *A Call To Joy* will want to continue their discipling relationship. With this in mind, we suggest that you contact your Coordinator to request *A Call To Growth* Discipler training. This training will prepare you to continue your equipping ministry. You and your Timothy may obtain these materials from the same source that provided *A Call To Joy*. In addition, as needed, you may use the resource information and toll free number provided on page 113. *A Call To Growth* includes eleven sessions and is designed to help your Timothy:

A. Learn principles for successfully dealing with *temptation*.

B. Understand and experience the *five* most basic aspects of prayer.

C. Learn the joy of spiritual *giving* out of a grateful heart.

D. Experience guided *Bible study* while focusing on these important subjects:

1. **New Life in Christ**
2. **Putting Christ First**
3. **The Devotional Life**
4. **Prayer and Dependency**
5. **God's Identity**
6. **Sharing Christ with Others**
7. **The Holy Spirit's Role in Our Lives**
8. **The Importance of God's Word**
9. **The Importance of the Church**

E. Enjoy doing *independent* Bible Study.

F. Share a clear witness using *three* different methods:

    1. **A Word of Truth**
    2. **A Personal Testimony**
    3. **The Bridge Illustration**

G. Gain *witnessing* experience through guided projects.

H. *Memorize* Scripture.

I. *Meditate* on Scripture.

SESSION ONE DISCIPLER'S DISCUSSION GUIDE

1

Discipler: It is *very important* that you carefully read "Preparing for Each Session" starting on page xvii. This material will help you understand how to lead each of these seven sessions.

Do not simply read the boxed material to your Timothy during the session. Highlight a key word so you can quickly glance at the sentence and deliver the question, amplification, or illustration. Always keep *good eye contact* with your Timothy.

1. **Get Acquainted:** Begin by briefly telling him something about your own family, occupation, school, personal interests, and favorite recreational activities. Invite him to share the same kind of information with you. (See page 197, #1) (Use the blanks provided if you have additional illustrations, amplifications, or questions for your Timothy).

2. "Let's read 'Welcome to *A Call To Joy*' aloud."

WELCOME TO *A CALL TO JOY*

In celebration of your desire to grow in the Christian life, you will not only receive this book, but much more importantly, receive a friend! Each time you meet together you can enjoy Christian fellowship. During your times of discussion, prayer, and Bible study, you will have the opportunity of knowing one another better.

Normally, it takes from seven to ten weeks to cover this inspirational material. We pray that these will be some of the most rewarding and enjoyable weeks you have ever experienced. James 4:8 says, *"Draw near to God and He will draw near to you."*

This first meeting will be very different from the rest because we want to be sure that a new church member has a clear understanding of what it means to know Christ as their personal Savior. We trust that you will be enriched by this basic study, even if you have already understood all or part of it's essential message.

1. Seek to determine your Timothy's relationship with Christ during this session. (See page 197, #2)

   _____

   _____

   _____

   _____

   _____

   _____

2. "Let's get right into our Bible study. Today we will focus on understanding the Gospel."

   _____

   _____

   _____

   _____

   _____

UNDERSTANDING THE GOSPEL

A. Mankind's Spiritual Need.

"As it is written, 'There is none righteous, not even one.'" (Romans 3:10)

The account of man's initial disobedience to God is recorded in Genesis 2 and 3.

1. *"And the Lord God commanded the man, 'You are free to eat from any tree in the garden; but you must not eat from the tree of the knowledge of good and evil, for when you eat of it you will surely die.'"* (Genesis 2:16 & 17, NIV)

> 1. "What was the *one* limitation which God placed on man-kind?"
>
> _____
>
> _____
>
> _____
>
> 2. "What did God say about the consequences of our spiritual disobedience?"
>
> _____
>
> _____
>
> _____

2. *"Therefore, just as through one man sin entered the world, and death through sin, and thus death spread to all men, because all sinned."* (Romans 5:12, NKJV)

> "How has Adam's sin affected the entire human race?"
>
> _____
>
> _____
>
> _____
>
> _____

3. *"For all have sinned and fall short of the glory of God."* (Romans 3:23)

> "Jesus Christ was sinless and has always been the Father's glorious standard of perfection. Can anyone's life ever measure up to His?"
>
> _____
>
> _____
>
> _____
>
> _____
>
> _____

B. Consequences of Disobedience.

Man chose to disobey God, and consequence always follows choice!

There are two kinds of death explained in the Bible. One is *physical*, which we will look at in a moment, and the other is *spiritual*, which the Bible is talking about in Romans 6:23.

1. *"For the wages of sin is death, but the gift of God is eternal life in Christ Jesus our Lord."* (Romans 6:23, NKJV)

> "A wage is something you *earn*, so spiritual death is actually deserved. This is why an unrepentant sinner who dies without Christ is eternally separated from God."
>
> _____
>
> _____
>
> _____
>
> _____
>
> _____

2. *"And as it is appointed for men to die once, but after this the judgement."* (Hebrews 9:27, NKJV)

> "According to the Bible, physical death is not the *end* of life. What awaits each person after death?"
>
> _____
>
> _____

C. God's Provision.

Man's sin called for *judgment*. Yet God's love for man called for *forgiveness*. God remained true to His character of being just and loving by paying sin's penalty Himself.

1. *"But God demonstrates His own love toward us, in that while we were still sinners, Christ died for us."* (Romans 5:8, NKJV)

> "How did God demonstrate His great love toward us as sinners?"
>
> _____
>
> _____

2. *"For Christ died for sins once for all, the righteous for the unrighteous, to bring you to God. He was put to death in the body but made alive by the Spirit."* (1 Peter 3:18, NIV)

> "What did Christ's death accomplish on our behalf?"
>
> _____
>
> _____

3. *"For by grace you have been saved through faith, and that not of yourselves; it is the gift of God, not of works, lest anyone should boast."* (Ephesians 2:8 & 9, NKJV)

> "What does Ephesians 2:8 & 9 teach regarding salvation?"
>
> _____
>
> _____

D. Man's Response.

Christ has come and revealed God. His death has satisfied God's righteousness and justice. Through Christ we can have our sins forgiven, be in right standing with God, and have eternal life. But we are not forced to believe or to accept God's mercy and grace. The choice is ours!

1. *"Now after John was put in prison, Jesus came to Galilee, preaching the gospel of the Kingdom of God, and saying, 'The time is fulfilled, and the kingdom of God is at hand. Repent, and believe in the gospel.'"* (Mark 1:14 & 15, NKJV)

---

1. "What response did Jesus *expect* and *require* from all those who wanted to be His disciples?"

   _____

   _____

2. "What does it mean to *repent?*"

   _____

   _____

---

2. *"Yet to all who <u>received</u> Him, to those who <u>believed</u> in His name, He gave the right to become children of God."* (John 1:12, NIV)

"What are the *two* steps described in this verse that explain how to become a child of God?"

   _____

   _____

Discipler: An underlined word in your Discipler's Guide indicates a blank space to be filled in by the Timothy in his book during each session.

---

3. You must ____believe____ and ____receive____ .

1. Read Isaiah 9:6. Point out that Jesus was the "Mighty God" revealed to us as man.
2. Next, read John 1:1 and 14; and briefly discuss the importance of the Trinity. Clearly identify Jesus the Savior, as God the Son.

First, you must *believe* that Jesus is *who* He claimed to be. He was born of a virgin, lived a sinless life, paid the penalty for our sins, and rose from the dead. He said He came to *seek* and *save* the lost, and to be our Savior.

Next, you must *receive* Him as your own personal Savior.

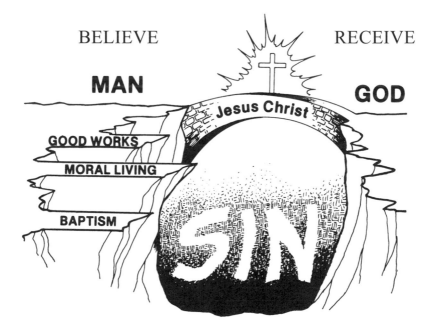

BELIEVE   RECEIVE

MAN   GOD

Jesus Christ

GOOD WORKS

MORAL LIVING

BAPTISM

SIN

"How does this drawing illustrate salvation?"

_____

_____

_____

_____

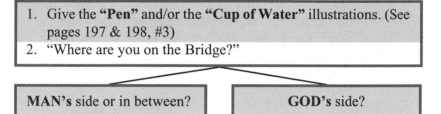

1. Give the **"Pen"** and/or the **"Cup of Water"** illustrations. (See pages 197 & 198, #3)
2. "Where are you on the Bridge?"

MAN's side or in between?	**GOD's** side?
1. "Do you believe that Jesus is *who* He claimed to be?" 2. "Good, that's the first step. Now would you like to take the next step and receive Him into your life as your Lord and Savior?" "Good!" (If he is not ready to receive Christ, see page 198, #4.)	Rejoice with him and explain the benefits of being a Christian here on earth as well as in heaven! Turn the page and keep going.

3. Explain the following "Prayer for Salvation."

"Lord Jesus, I am a sinner, . . .	**Confession**
but I am sorry for my sins.	**Contrition**
I want to turn from my sins; I am willing to begin a new life with Your help.	**Repentance**
Lord Jesus, please come into my heart and life right now.	**Invitation**
From this moment forward, my life belongs to You and You alone.	**Consecration**
I will love You, serve You, tell others about You, and trust You to live Your life through me.	**Dependence**
Thank You Lord, for coming into my life and for forgiving my sins today."	**Thanksgiving**

1. "There is no magic in the particular words of this prayer, for receiving Christ is an act of your will. This prayer simply reflects the inward decision you are making."
2. Lead him in "A Prayer for Salvation."
3. Congratulate and welcome him into God's family!

4. *"He who has the Son has life; he who does not have the Son of God does not have life. These things I have written to you who believe in the name of the Son of God, that you may know that you have eternal life, and that you may continue to believe in the name of the Son of God."* (1 John 5:12 & 13, NKJV)

5. *"For God so loved the world that He gave His only begotten Son, that whoever believes in Him should not perish but have everlasting life."* (John 3:16, NKJV)

6. *"In Him we have redemption through His blood, the forgiveness of sins, according to the riches of His grace."* (Ephesians 1:7, NKJV)

---

1. "From the previous three verses, what does God the Father promise to those who believe in God the Son?"
2. "What does the word 'know' in 1 John 5:13 tell us about our assurance of eternal life?"

Although man was created without knowledge of evil, he yielded to Satan's temptation and chose to know both good and evil. The consequence of this choice was spiritual death – separation from God. God's response was to judge mankind for disobedience and provide salvation through Christ. By receiving Christ, a person receives forgiveness of sin and becomes a child of God for eternity!

---

1. Explain the difference Christ has made in your own life.
2. Tell about the other people that have helped you grow spiritually.
3. Explain the purpose of *A Call To Joy*:
   "*A Call To Joy* will give you the practical tools needed for spiritual growth." (See page 199, #5)
4. Together, turn to the first Quiet Time on page 78.
5. Explain that each morning your Timothy can enjoy a Quiet Time reading and a time of Scriptural insight and prayer.
6. One of the most important concepts that you will be teaching throughout *A Call To Joy* is how to have an effective daily

Quiet Time. When you teach him this process, he will be able to experience consistent growth long after your meetings have concluded. Because of this priority, we have included the opportunity to exchange Quiet Time insights at the start of each session.

7   "Be sure to write down any questions from your Quiet Time reading and we will discuss them next week."
8. "Do you think you can go to bed 15 minutes earlier tonight so you can spend 15 minutes with God tomorrow morning?"

USING THE NOTE-TAKING SECTION OF YOUR *SPIRITUAL JOURNAL*

"How much of last Sunday's sermon do you remember? Taking sermon notes helps us *remember* Biblical concepts so we can *apply* them to our daily lives."

Psychologists tell us that after 72 hours, we normally remember:

Only about __10%__ of what we hear.
Only about __30%__ of what we read.
About __50%__ of what we hear and read.
About __90%__ of what we hear, read, and do!

This study was conducted by the United States Air Force.

1. "You can see from these statistics how taking notes will greatly increase your retention level. You will be able to grow spiritually more quickly if you *retain* the insights you receive from pastors and teachers."
2. "Let's read and discuss the note-taking section of the *Spiritual Journal*, pages 46 & 47."

THE IMPORTANCE OF BECOMING INVOLVED IN A LOCAL CHURCH

1. *"And they were continually devoting themselves to the apostles' teaching and to fellowship, to the breaking of bread and to prayer."* (Acts 2:42)

> "What should Christians continually devote themselves to?"
>
> _____
>
> _____

2. *"Let us not give up meeting together, as some are in the habit of doing, but let us encourage one another – and all the more as you see the Day approaching."* (Hebrews 10:25, NIV)

> "What does this verse teach us?"
>
> _____
>
> _____

3. *"And He gave some as apostles, and some as prophets, and some as evangelists, and some as pastors and teachers, for the equipping of the saints for the work of service, to the building up of the body of Christ."* (Ephesians 4:11 & 12)

> 1. "God has given many people the special responsibility of equipping the saints through preaching, teaching, and training. We are to be equipped so we can grow spiritually and minister to others."
> 2. "Are you going to be able to attend this week's worship service?"
> 3. "Why don't we try to sit together?"
> 4. "How about going to lunch together after the service?"
> 5. Emphasize the importance of small group Bible study. Encourage your Timothy to enroll in a new believers/new members class or Sunday Bible study. If needed, offer to attend the first session with him.
> 6. "Where would you like to meet for next week's session?"
> 7. "Do you have a modern translation of the Bible which you find easy to understand?"
> 8. "Be sure to bring your Bible, pen, and study materials to next week's session."
> 9. "Let's review your Weekly Spiritual Growth Assignment."

TIMOTHY'S WEEKLY SPIRITUAL GROWTH ASSIGNMENT:

Timothy: You will notice that your book contains several blanks. These blanks are to be filled in *during each session* with your Discipler, not as a homework assignment.

A. Read a Quiet Time each morning this week, starting on page 78. Mark highlights as you read and be prepared to share them next week. You may wish to mark highlights by putting an "*" at the start of a highlight, and a ")" at the end. Pray the suggested prayer to God at the end of your Quiet Time. You may wish to pray this prayer aloud.

B. Read Chapter 1, "The Love of God," starting on page 39. Mark highlights as you read and be prepared to share them next week.

C. Take sermon notes using your *Spiritual Journal* and be prepared to share highlights next week. If you have questions about the sermon, be sure to write them down. You can ask your Discipler about them during your next session.

D. Start reading the Gospel of John *at your own pace*. If you have any questions as you read, write them in the note-taking section of your *Spiritual Journal*. Ask your Discipler to answer them during your next session.

Close with prayer thanking God for the opportunity to deepen your relationship with one another and with Him.

Discipler: You will be completing both the Timothy's Assignment and Discipler's Assignment each week. However, you need not cover the same Quiet Times as your Timothy if you are currently using a different Bible reading schedule.

DISCIPLER'S WEEKLY SPIRITUAL GROWTH ASSIGNMENT:

Read Chapter 6, "Follow-Up, An Overview," starting on page 119.

SESSION TWO DISCIPLER'S FELLOWSHIP GUIDE

2

Discipler: Your Timothy may have questions from his reading in the Gospel of John. If he does, take the necessary time to answer each one. Remember that covering this material at the suggested rate of speed is not important compared with meeting the spiritual needs of your Timothy.

During the next few sessions, you will be encouraging your Timothy to prayerfully give a copy of *Steps to Peace with God* to a friend or acquaintance. If you are meeting in restaurants, you can provide a good example by giving a booklet to your new server each week. Simply say something like this:

"I know that you are busy right now, but when you have a chance, maybe you can read this Christian booklet. It tells how to have a personal relationship with God. Having that relationship has brought me real peace and joy! If you have any questions, my phone number is on the back."

1. **Informal Conversation** – Use this time to deepen your friendship. You can do this by showing your interest in his overall life and activities.
2. **Inspiration** – Share at least one personal spiritual experience from your week.

DISCUSS LAST WEEK'S ASSIGNMENTS

1. Ask him to share a highlight from each daily Quiet Time.
2. "During the next week, you will be reading a Quiet Time and then writing a Scriptural insight and prayer each morning."
3. "Let's do a sample Quiet Time together and write out a Scriptural insight and prayer. We can use Quiet Time #8 on page 85."
4. Make sure your Timothy knows how to find books, chapters, and verses in the Bible.
5. Read a favorite Quiet Time from your own Journal.
6. Exchange highlights from your sermon notes.
7. Discuss highlights from Chapter 1, "The Love of God."

WHAT DOES THE BIBLE SAY ABOUT SALVATION?

A. **1 John 5:11-13:** *"And the witness is this, that God has given us eternal life, and this life is in His Son. He who has the Son has the life; he who does not have the Son of God does not have the life. These things I have written to you who believe in the name of the Son of God, in order that you may know that you have eternal life."*

God wants you to *know for certain* that you are a Christian!

Give the **"Marriage Illustration."** (See page 199, #6)
(Ask your Timothy to fill in the blanks of his book as you work through each session.)

_____

B. **There is a difference between** _____relationship_____ **and** _____fellowship_____.

Give the **"Young Man Who Runs Away From Home"** illustration. (See page 199, #7)

ILLUSTRATION:__The Young Man Who Runs Away From Home__.

When I am out of fellowship with God, I may have false __doubts__.

1. "In John 8:44, Jesus called Satan the 'Father of Lies.'"
2. "Satan delights in . . ." (See page 200, #8)
3. "Legitimate guilt is brought . . ." (See page 200, #8)
4. "Let's turn to 1 John 1:9 and find out what to do if legitimate guilt occurs."
5. "Non-legitimate guilt can occur from. . ." (See page 200, #8)
6. "Feelings are important, but . . ." (See page 200, #8)

We need to _____ trust God in faith _____ and accept __His__ promise, rather than our feelings as the basis for our assurance of salvation.

1. Give a personal example about your own assurance.
2. Give the **"Ruth Graham"** illustration. (See page 200, #9)

ILLUSTRATION: _____ Ruth Graham _____

We can __trust__ in God's forgiveness and __rejoice__ in His salvation!

HOW DO I SHARE MY DECISION WITH FAMILY AND FRIENDS?

"How did your family and friends react when you became a Christian?"

Be ____ consistent ____ and __gentle__.

"Don't be overly aggressive when giving your witness. Your family needs to *see your walk* as clearly as they *hear your talk*."

Billy Graham has said, "The true test of every Christian is the way he_____lives at home_____."

> 1. "We need to maintain strong family relationships while developing our Christian convictions."
> 2. "Is anyone in your family not yet a Christian?"
> 3. "Why don't we stop right now and pray for them?"
> 4. Briefly, show your Timothy how to use the *Steps to Peace with God* booklet.

WHAT IS A DAILY QUIET TIME?

DEFINITION: A Quiet Time is a part of your day which is set aside for _____fellowship with God_____. It normally includes Bible reading, prayer, and a decision to apply a Scriptural insight.

> "Nutritionists tell us that breakfast is the most important meal of the day. Why? Because we need physical nourishment to get started in the morning. In the same way, we need spiritual nourishment at the beginning of our day."

Psalm 46:10a says, *"Be still, and know that I am God . . ."* (KJV)

> 1. "Does 'being still' come naturally for you?"
> 2. Give the **"Driving Around the Pumps"** illustration. (See page 200, #10)

ILLUSTRATION:_____Driving Around the Pumps_____.

Our daily danger is becoming ___too busy___ for God to *bless* us!

WHY HAVE A DAILY QUIET TIME?

A. To help fulfill your highest purpose.

> "Genesis 1:27 says that man was created in God's own image. This means that we were created with the capacity to enjoy *spiritual fellowship*. In all of creation, no one but man enjoys this amazing privilege!"

"God is faithful, through whom you were called into fellowship with His Son, Jesus Christ our Lord." (1 Corinthians 1:9)

Every Christian has a high calling: ____fellowship____ with Christ!

B. To follow the Lord's example.

> "Jesus never let his busy schedule keep Him from spending time alone in prayer."
>
> _____
>
> _____

"Very early in the morning, while it was still dark, Jesus got up, left the house and went off to a solitary place, where He prayed." (Mark 1:35, NIV)

> "The busier His schedule became, the more committed He was to spending time alone with His Father."
>
> _____
>
> _____

"Yet the news about Him spread all the more, so that crowds of people came to hear Him and to be healed of their sicknesses. But Jesus often withdrew to lonely places and prayed." (Luke 5:15 & 16, NIV)

For the Lord Jesus, having Quiet Times was an absolute ____priority____.

> *"The greater the demands on our lives, the greater our need to spend time alone with God.* Martin Luther, the great Christian Reformer once said, 'I have so much to do today, I must begin with at least two hours alone with God.'"
>
> _____

C. To gain spiritual strength.

> "Daily food is *not an option* if we desire to be physically strong, and spiritual food is *not an option* if we desire to be spiritually strong. This is why it is important not to skip our spiritual meals."
>
> _____
>
> _____

"I have not departed from the commandment of His lips; I have treasured the words of His mouth more than my necessary food." (Job 23:12, NKJV)

> "Job thought more of God's Word than he did of food. How important is the Bible to you?"
>
> _____
>
> _____

Jesus said, *"Man does not live by bread alone, but on every word that comes from the mouth of God."* (Matthew 4:4b, NIV)

> "What is the central teaching of this verse? If that is true, how should it affect the way we prioritize our time?"
>
> _____
>
> _____

The Bible is our source of spiritual _____ strength _____ and _____ wisdom _____.

> "Let's review this week's Spiritual Growth Assignment."

TIMOTHY'S WEEKLY SPIRITUAL GROWTH ASSIGNMENT:

A. Continue reading your Quiet Times each morning. Start writing a Scriptural insight and prayer for each day. Be prepared to share them next week.

B. Read Chapter 2, "Learning to Walk," starting on page 45. Mark highlights as you read and be prepared to share them next week.

C. Take sermon notes using your *Spiritual Journal* and be prepared to share highlights next week.

D. Read *Steps to Peace with God* and stop to thank Him for your personal salvation!

E. Continue reading the Gospel of John at your own pace.

1. "Do you have any special prayer needs for this coming week?"
2. "Let's take turns and pray conversationally together."
3. Explain that God looks upon our hearts, and is more concerned about our sincerity than the specific words which we use in prayer. Next, point out that in conversational prayer, we simply pray back and forth as we feel led, expressing one phrase or sentence at a time.

DISCIPLER'S WEEKLY SPIRITUAL GROWTH ASSIGNMENT:

Read Chapter 7, "Developing A Meaningful Relationship," starting on page 137.

SESSION THREE
DISCIPLER'S
FELLOWSHIP
GUIDE

3

Informal Conversation: Ask your Timothy about his week. Be sure to inquire about any special subjects which you prayed about together last week. If you learn that an unusual temptation or stressful situation has been present, plan ahead to call as often as needed and briefly pray together about the problem. (See page 200, #11)

_____

_____

_____

_____

_____

_____

_____

DISCUSS LAST WEEK'S ASSIGNMENTS

1. "Did you enjoy your Quiet Times this past week?"
2. Ask your Timothy to share his favorite Scriptural insights and prayers from this week's Quiet Times.
3. "During this next week, you will be reading a short Scripture passage, Quiet Time reading, and then writing your insights, prayers, and applications."
4. "An application is something that the Lord is leading you to actually *do* as a result of your Scriptural insight and prayer."
5. "Let's do a sample Quiet Time together and write out a Scriptural insight, prayer, and application. We can use Quiet Time #16 on page 93."
6. Share one or two of your own Quiet Times.
7. Exchange highlights from sermon notes.
8. Discuss highlights from Chapter 2, "Learning To Walk."

WHAT ARE THE PRACTICAL BENEFITS OF NOTE-TAKING?

"So then faith comes by hearing, and hearing by the word of God." (Romans 10:17, NKJV)

A. My faith_____grows_____ each time I hear God's Word.

B. We take notes because of a basic human problem — _____forgetfulness_____.

1. Give the **"Leaky Bucket"** illustration. (See page 201, #12)
2. "Using your *Spiritual Journal* for notes each Sunday will help you patch the leaks in your memory."
3. "The more of God's Word you *retain,* the more you will have to *apply!*"
4. "The most important part of any sermon or Bible study is its personal application."

ILLUSTRATION: _____Leaky Bucket_____.

Note-taking helps you:

1. _____Listen_____ more intently.

2. _____Retain_____ what you hear.

3. _____Apply_____ the message to your life.

4. _____Share_____ the truth with others.

YOU CAN DEVELOP AN EFFECTIVE DAILY QUIET TIME

A. By discovering its practical benefits for yourself.

1. It is a key to fulfilling _____God's plan_____ for your life.

*"Do not let this Book of the Law depart from your mouth;
meditate on it day and night, so that you may be careful to
do everything written in it. Then you will be prosperous and
successful."* (Joshua 1:8, NIV)

---

1. "Our daily Quiet Times help us *understand* and then *apply*
    God's Word in everyday life!"
2. "True success is *finding* and *fulfilling* God's will by using
    the gifts which He has given us. Ephesians 2:10 says, *'For
    we are God's workmanship, created in Christ Jesus to do
    good works, which God prepared in advance for us to do.'"*
    (NIV)

_____

_____

_____

_____

_____

---

2. It is the means used by The Holy Spirit to reveal the
    _____actions_____ , _____attitudes_____ or _____priorities_____
    in your life which He wants to help you develop or change.

King David prayed, *"Search me, O God, and know my heart; test me and know my anxious thoughts. See if there is any offensive way in me, and lead me in the way everlasting."* (Psalm 139: 23 & 24 , NIV)

Tell your Timothy about a special time when God used your own Quiet Time to reveal a personal need or spiritual opportunity. Next, tell him about the *joy* you experienced when you acted in obedience. This openness and humility will help deepen the level of trust and reality in your friendship.

_____

_____

_____

_____

3. It prepares you to be used in the lives of ____others____.

"When they saw the courage of Peter and John and realized that they were unschooled, ordinary men, they were astonished and they took note that these men had been with Jesus." (Acts 4:13, NIV)

1. "When you spend consistent time with God, it will become evident to those around you. Your life will be characterized by inner peace and God-given strength."
2. "As you grow spiritually, ministering to others will become natural. Every one of us is important in God's plan for winning, training, and encouraging others."

_____

_____

_____

_____

4. It provides the opportunity for ____fellowship____ with our Lord.

> Jesus said, *". . . I am with you always, to the very end of the age."* (Matthew 28:20, NIV)

---

1. "Throughout history, Christians have enjoyed the privilege of fellowship with the Lord Jesus through the ministry of the Holy Spirit."
2. "We can enjoy Quiet Times with Him anywhere, at any time, and always be assured that He is there."

_____

_____

B. By anticipating your Quiet Times in faith!

1. _____Expect_____ God to meet with you and guide you through ____His Word____.

    "I will instruct you and teach you in the way you should go." (Psalm 32:8a, NIV)

"The Bible provides the best counsel available for making wise daily decisions, so we need to read it!"

> *"Thy word is a lamp to my feet, and a light to my path."* (Psalm 119:105)

"His guidance is available to us morning by morning."

> *"He awakens me morning by morning, He awakens my ear to listen as a disciple."* (Isaiah 50:4b)

1. "Isn't it wonderful to know that the same God who made us stands ready to teach and lead us every morning?"
2. "He never fails to *bless* us when we are faithful to meet with Him."

2. Determine to be ____consistent____.

> 1. Give the **"Good Athlete"** illustration. (See page 201, #13)
> 2. "It is better to faithfully meet with God for a few minutes every day than to be inconsistent and then suddenly decide to spend an extended time with Him."
> 3. "Disciplined consistency leads to spiritual growth!"

ILLUSTRATION: _____A Good Athlete_____.

The apostle Paul said, *". . . discipline yourself for the purpose of godliness."* (1 Timothy 4:7b)

> "We gain spiritual strength for effective ministry through our fellowship with God. This is why daily Quiet Times are so important."

"Let us not grow weary while doing good, for in due season we shall reap if we do not lose heart." (Galatians 6:9, NKJV)

> Give the **"You Don't Quit Eating"** illustration. (See page 201, #14)

ILLUSTRATION: _____You Don't Quit Eating_____.

3. Always ____Apply____ the insights God gives you during your Quiet Time.

"Do not merely listen to the word, and so deceive yourselves. Do what it says." (James 1:22, NIV)

> "The Lord will provide His *direction* and *correction* as you seek to do His will!"

You can expect His correction to include:

a. _____Activities_____ you either need to *start or stop*.

b. _____Attitudes_____ you need to either *develop or change*.

C. By planning ahead for success.

1. Get a good night's _____rest_____, so you wake up refreshed.

   "How long will you lie there, you sluggard? When will you get up from your sleep?" (Proverbs 6:9, NIV)

> 1. "You *cannot* stay up late at night and feel like having a good Quiet Time early the next morning."
> 2. "If you hoot with the owls, you cannot soar with the eagles!"

2. _____Start_____ your day with Christ!

   David, the Psalmist, said, *"In the morning, O Lord, You hear my voice."* (Psalm 5:3a, NIV)

> 1. "Give God the best part of your day. Normally this will be in the morning, when you are the freshest. Our attitude about the day is usually established in the morning."
> 2. "Think about these questions:
>   • Would a *violinist* play in a concert without tuning his instrument?
>   • Would a *pilot* make his flight without talking to the control tower?
>   • Would a *Christian* seek to serve Christ without asking for His guidance?"

3. Select a special _____place_____.

> 1. "Avoid distractions by rising early when the house is quiet."
> 2. "Select a place that:
>   • is convenient
>   • has a pleasant atmosphere.
>   • has good lighting."
> 3. "Using the same location each morning will help you build a successful pattern and attitude of expectancy."
> 4. Describe the place where you have your own personal Quiet Time.

HOW DO YOU SUSTAIN YOUR PERSONAL DISCIPLINE AND GROWTH?

"He who walks with wise men will be wise. . ." (Proverbs 13:20a)

> 1. "It is a proven fact that we want to be with those whom we admire. Who has been your best spiritual influence in recent years?"
> 2. Give the **"Redwood Trees"** illustration. (See page 202, #15)

ILLUSTRATION:＿＿＿＿＿＿＿＿Redwood Trees＿＿＿＿＿＿＿＿.

Remember that growth comes ＿＿＿slowly＿＿＿ , so be patient and enjoy each new day of fellowship with God and other Christians.

> 1. "Focus on a key word or phrase from your Quiet Time and carry it with you throughout the day."
> 2. "Pray to find a Christian friend who can be a prayer partner. The fellowship will encourage you both!"
> 3. "Let's review your Spiritual Growth Assignment for the week."

TIMOTHY'S WEEKLY SPIRITUAL GROWTH ASSIGNMENT:

A. Continue your daily Quiet Times each morning. Write a Scriptural insight, prayer, and application for each day. Be prepared to share them next week.

B. Read Chapter 3, "The Perfect Example," starting on page 53. Mark highlights for discussion next week.

C. Take sermon notes using your *Spiritual Journal,* and come prepared to share your favorite highlights.

D. Continue reading the Gospel of John at your own pace.

> "Let's close with Prayer."

> ### DISCIPLER'S WEEKLY SPIRITUAL GROWTH ASSIGNMENT:
>
> Read Chapter 8, "A New Testament Approach to Ministry," starting on page 151.

SESSION FOUR DISCIPLER'S DISCUSSION GUIDE

4

1. **Informal Conversation:** "After your first three weeks of enjoying a daily Quiet Time, how would you describe the changes that are taking place in your attitudes?"
2. "Now that you have been a church member for several weeks, what excites you most about the church's ministry?"
3. Find out if he is making *friends* naturally and be sure to help if he is not.
4. If he shows a spontaneous interest in an activity or ministry of the church, prayerfully encourage that interest.

_____

_____

_____

_____

DISCUSS LAST WEEK'S ASSIGNMENTS

1. Ask him to tell you about his favorite Scriptural insights and applications from each daily Quiet Time during this past week.
2. Share one of your own new Quiet Time insights.
3. "Let's turn to page 101 in your *Timothy's Guide*. Notice that there are no more blanks to fill in at the bottom of the page."
4. "Now let's turn to page 20 in your *Spiritual Journal*. You will continue reading the Quiet Times in your *Timothy's Guide*, however, you can now start writing your insights, prayers, and applications in your own *Spiritual Journal*."
5. Exchange highlights from sermon notes.
6. Discuss highlights from Chapter 3, "The Perfect Example."

THE PRIVILEGE OF SHARING GOD'S GOOD NEWS

"The following verses focus on God's commission for us to share Christ with others in the power of the Holy Spirit."

_____

_____

"Therefore go and make disciples of all nations, baptizing them in the name of the Father and of the Son and of the Holy Spirit, and teaching them to obey everything I have commanded you. And surely I am with you always, to the very end of the age." (Matthew 28:19 & 20, NIV)

"But you will receive power when the Holy Spirit comes on you; and you will be My witnesses in Jerusalem, and in all Judea and Samaria, and to the ends of the earth." (Acts 1:8, NIV)

"Let's look at the benefit of using an evangelistic booklet such as *Steps to Peace with God*."

_____

_____

Using an evangelistic booklet:

A. **Keeps you focused on the** ____subject____.

B. **Insures the availability of** ____important verses____.

C. **Allows the inquirer to** __review__ **the message.**

D. **Provides** __visual__ **assistance to underscore the verbal message.**

> 1. "You can say something like this, in your own words, when you give the booklet away:
>   'I know that you are busy right now, but when you have a chance, maybe you can read this Christian booklet. It tells how to have a personal relationship with God. Having that relationship has brought me real peace and joy! If you have any questions, my phone number is on the back.'"
> 2. "This booklet has already helped thousands come to faith in Christ and it may be just what someone needs."
> 3. "Do you have a friend or family member who still needs to know Christ? For a moment, let's imagine that *you* are that person, and I will briefly explain the booklet."
> 4. Next, reverse roles and let your Timothy present the booklet to you.

THE PRIVILEGE OF PRAYER

A. **The nature of prayer.**

Prayer has been defined as "Man's conversation with God."

> "Jesus taught us to pray with great simplicity." (Matthew 6:9-13)
> Give the **"Billy Graham"** illustration. (See page 202, #16)

ILLUSTRATION: ____Billy Graham____.

1. Through prayer, we can talk with God about
    _____anything_____ , _____anytime_____ ,
    _____anywhere_____ .

> "When a Christian says that God has spoken to him, he is
> typically referring to an inner voice which others cannot hear.
> This is the voice of the Holy Spirit."

2. Prayer involves both ____speaking____ and ____listening____
    to God.

B. The Lord Jesus' prayer life.

> "Let's read and discuss the following verses."

1. He prayed in the _____morning_____ .

*"Very early in the morning, while it was still dark, Jesus got
up, left the house and went off to a solitary place, where He
prayed."* (Mark 1:35, NIV)

> "The house Mark is speaking about in this verse was located in
> Capernaum, and it belonged to Peter's mother-in-law. The Lord
> was very tired because of the previous day's ministry, but He got
> up early to be alone for His Quiet Time."

2. He prayed _____consistently_____ .

*"Yet the news about Him spread all the more, so that crowds
of people came to hear Him and to be healed of their
sicknesses. But Jesus often withdrew to lonely places and
prayed."* (Luke 5:15 & 16, NIV)

> 1. "No one has ever had a greater reason to say, 'I'm too busy
>   to pray today.' The Lord was literally pressed and sur-
>   rounded by human need, yet He consistently carved islands
>   in His day for time alone with the Father."
> 2. "If Jesus needed to do this, how much more do you and I?"

3. He earnestly prayed ___before___ making major decisions.

"One of those days Jesus went out to a mountainside to pray, and spent the night praying to God. When morning came, He called His disciples to Him and chose twelve of them, whom He also designated apostles." (Luke 6:12 & 13, NIV)

---

1. "Our important decisions in life may call for consistent and intense prayer. The Lord did not pray all night on a regular basis, but on this occasion, He was choosing the men who would affect the destiny of Christianity and the future salvation of billions of people."
2. "If all the apostles had been unfaithful like Judas, you and I would be lost, spiritually empty, and hopeless today. We can praise God for selecting a team of faithful men and women who witnessed and passed the Gospel message from one generation to the next!"

_____

_____

C. Make prayer a consistent priority of your life.

1. Prayer is an alternative to ___worry___.

"Do not be anxious about anything, but in everything, by prayer and petition, with thanksgiving, present your requests to God." (Philippians 4:6, NIV)

2. Prayer is a means of avoiding ___temptation___.

"Watch and pray so that you will not fall into temptation. The spirit is willing, but the body is weak." (Matthew 26:41, NIV)

3. Prayer is a means of great ___accomplishment___.

"The prayer of a righteous man is powerful and effective." (James 5:16b, NIV)

"Let's look at this coming week's Spiritual Growth Assignment."

TIMOTHY'S WEEKLY SPIRITUAL GROWTH ASSIGNMENT:

A. Continue your daily Quiet Times using your *Timothy's Guide* and *Spiritual Journal.* Be prepared to share your insights next week.

B. Prayerfully give a copy of *Steps to Peace with God* to someone this week. If they seem open to talk, simply pray silently for guidance and let the conversation develop naturally.

C. Read Chapter 4, "The Secret of Godliness," starting on page 59. Mark highlights and be prepared to share them next week.

D. Take sermon notes using your *Spiritual Journal.* Be prepared to discuss your highlights next week.

E. Continue reading the Gospel of John at your own pace.

1. "Let's turn to page 14 in our *Spiritual Journals,* and exchange prayer requests. This way we can pray specifically for one another each morning this week."
2. "It's time to close this session, so let's pray for one another before we part."

DISCIPLER'S WEEKLY SPIRITUAL GROWTH ASSIGNMENT:

Read Chapter 9, "Association with Jesus," starting on page 161.

SESSION FIVE DISCIPLER'S DISCUSSION GUIDE

5

Informal Discussion:
1. "How did your week go?"
2. "Did you have the opportunity to give *Steps to Peace with God* to someone? Tell me about it."
3. "You probably noticed that you have completed the Quiet Time readings in your book. From now on, you will be reading directly from the Bible to receive your Scriptural insights."
4. "Let's read and discuss pages 6 & 7 in our *Spiritual Journals*."
5. "Now, lct's read and discuss page 109 of the Quiet Time Reading Guide."
6. Next, ask your Timothy to find several possible Scriptural insights, prayers, and applications from the first chapter of Ephesians. This will show him how to have Quiet Times using his own Bible.

DISCUSS LAST WEEK'S ASSIGNMENT

1. Ask him to share his Scriptural insights, prayers, and applications from each Quiet Time this past week.
2. Share one of your own Quiet Times.
3. Exchange highlights from your sermon notes.
4. Discuss highlights from Chapter 4, "The Secret of Godliness."

DEVELOPING A LIFE OF PEACE THROUGH PRAYER

A. Maintain a proper attitude.

1. "The Bible has often been called a love letter from God. It expresses His grace, kindness, and the desire for us to be conformed to the image and character of His Son."
2. "Prayer is best understood as life's highest privilege, because it involves a conversation between our hearts and His."
3. "Perhaps the overarching attitude for effective prayer is humility. We are actually ushered into God's presence each time we pray, so our hearts need to be tender, and our minds need to be aware of who He really is."
4. "Let's look at several necessary *attitudes* for effective prayer."

   1. Be honest and transparent when you pray.

   "All my longings lie open before You, O Lord; my sighing is not hidden from You." (Psalm 38:9, NIV)

   David knew that _____nothing_____ in his life was hidden from God.

1. "He talked to Him with complete openness. We need to be equally open and transparent when we pray."
2. Give your Timothy a personal example to illustrate this important aspect of prayer. This is your opportunity to explain that daily confession, cleansing, and humility are vital for happiness and inner peace (1 John 1:9).

   2. Keep your prayers simple.

"'Abba, Father, all things are possible unto Thee; take away this cup from Me: nevertheless not what I will, but what Thou wilt.'" (Mark 14:36, KJV)

God wants us to talk to Him with the same sincerity that a child expresses toward his loving _____father_____.

"When Jesus prayed in His darkest hour, He called God, 'Abba,' which literally means, 'Daddy' or 'Father.' This was the same affectionate expression that a Hebrew child used when speaking to his earthly father."

_____

_____

_____

---

3. Pray with pure motives.

"When you ask, you do not receive, because you ask with wrong motives . . ." (James 4:3a, NIV)

"All a man's ways seem innocent to him, but motives are weighed by the Lord." (Proverbs 16:2, NIV)

Our prayers are no better than _____our motives_____ for praying.

---

1. "To help determine if your motives are right when you pray, ask yourself this question, 'Is it my desire to *know* and do God's will, and to *bring Him glory?'*"

2. Give a personal example of praying with the right motive and with the wrong motive. Be as practical as possible.

_____

_____

_____

B. Make prayer a natural part of your life.

1. Pray _____throughout_____ the day.

   "Pray continually." (1 Thessalonians 5:17, NIV)

   > "This requires developing a conscious *awareness* of God. It does *not* mean literally verbalizing prayer every minute of the day. Your spiritual objective is to maintain a frame of mind that allows Christ-centered thoughts and prayers to be natural and spontaneous whatever you may be doing."
   >
   > _____
   >
   > _____
   >
   > _____
   >
   > _____

2. It has been wisely said that a Christian will either pray for _____guidance_____ throughout the day or____forgiveness____ at night!

3. We need to ____ask____ before ____acting____, and pray about both _____large_____ and _____small_____ needs.

   "Do not be anxious about anything, but in everything, by prayer and petition, with thanksgiving, present your requests to God. And the peace of God, which transcends all understanding, will guard your hearts and your minds in Christ Jesus." (Philippians 4:6 & 7, NIV)

   > Give the **"Missionary in Africa"** illustration. (See page 202, #17)
   >
   > _____
   >
   > _____
   >
   > _____
   >
   > _____

   ILLUSTRATION: _____Missionary in Africa_____.

4. Pray _____specifically_____, in faith.

> *"And she made a vow, saying, 'O Lord Almighty, if You will only look upon Your servant's misery and remember me, and not forget Your servant but give her a son, then I will give him to the Lord for all the days of his life, and no razor will ever be used on his head.'"* (1 Samuel 1:11, NIV)

"When you pray in a general manner like, 'God please bless everyone,' or 'Lord help all the sick people,' it is difficult to ever give Him glory for answered prayer."

_____

_____

_____

Vague universal prayers make it _____difficult_____ to _____recognize_____ and appreciate God's answers.

C. Learn the Biblical guidelines for prayer.

> *"If My people, who are called by My name, will humble themselves and pray and seek My face and turn from their wicked ways, then will I hear from heaven and will forgive their sin and will heal their land."* (2 Chronicles 7:14, NIV)

"What is required for effective prayer?"

_____

_____

_____

> *"If I had cherished sin in my heart, the Lord would not have listened."* (Psalm 66:18, NIV)

We must desire and seek a clean _____heart_____ in preparation for a life of effective prayer.

D. Appreciate the different dimensions of prayer.

1. "Let's read and discuss the five basic aspects of prayer described on pages 9-13 of our *Spiritual Journals*." (Ask your Timothy to read every other paragraph.)
2. Read the following sample prayers and ask your Timothy to identify each one.

"Lord I am deeply humbled by the thought that You love me. As I meditate upon who You really are: Your unlimited knowledge, Your glory, and Your majesty, I count it life's greatest joy and privilege to be Your child!"

1.   Adoration   - Praising God for who He is.

"Father, I recognize that I have acted apart from Your will and that You hate sin. Please forgive me for _____. Thank You for the peace and mercy You have promised. I'm so glad You have taken away my guilt."

2.   Confession   - Agreeing with God about your sin.

"Thank You for the close friendship You have given me with _____ . I am truly grateful to know someone who shares my Christian values and enjoys serving You."

3.   Thanksgiving   - Thanking God for what He has done.

"Father, may the communication difficulties between Bill and Susan be resolved this week. Please restore their happy marriage."

4.   Intercession   - Praying for the needs of others.

> "Lord, please make me aware of the spiritual needs of my fellow workers on the job today, and give me the opportunity and boldness to talk to Mike about his relationship with You. Dear Lord, I also need the wisdom to handle my child's rebellious attitude at home."

5. _____Petition_____ - Praying for your personal needs.

> 1. Discuss your own commitment to prayer.
> 2. "It has been said, 'The man who fails to plan, plans to fail.' We need to plan ahead and establish a victorious life of prayer."

TIMOTHY'S WEEKLY SPIRITUAL GROWTH ASSIGNMENT:

A. Continue your daily Quiet Times using your *Spiritual Journal*, Bible, and Quiet Time Reading Guide on page 109. Be prepared to share your insights next week.

B. Give another copy of *Steps to Peace with God* to someone this week.

C. Read Chapter 5, "Principles for Living in Victory," starting on page 67. Mark highlights and be prepared to share them next week.

D. Take sermon notes using your *Spiritual Journal*. Be prepared to share your highlights next week.

E. List the name of one individual or ministry for each day of the week using the Intercession Section of your *Spiritual Journal* on pages 14-17.

F. Continue reading the Gospel of John at your own pace.

Close with prayers of adoration to our Lord.

DISCIPLER'S WEEKLY SPIRITUAL GROWTH ASSIGNMENT:

Read Chapter 10, "The Need For Multiplying Disciples," starting on page 173.

SESSION SIX
DISCIPLER'S
DISCUSSION
GUIDE

6

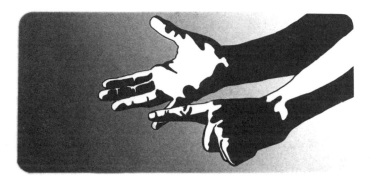

DISCUSS LAST WEEK'S ASSIGNMENTS

1. "Did you have a chance to give *Steps to Peace with God* to someone? Tell me about it."
2. Ask him to share his Scriptural insights, prayers, and applications from each Quiet Time this past week.
3. Share one of your Quiet Times.
4. Exchange highlights from your sermon notes.
5. Discuss highlights from Chapter 5, "Principles for Living in Victory."

_____
_____
_____
_____

THE MINISTRY OF THE HOLY SPIRIT

"I have been crucified with Christ; and it is no longer I who live, but Christ lives in me; and the life which I now live in the flesh I live by faith in the Son of God, who loved me, and delivered Himself up for me." (Galatians 2:20)

God is a Trinity consisting of God the Father, God the Son, and God the Holy Spirit. It is through the ministry of the Holy Spirit that Christ indwells believers and empowers us for Christian service.

"For it is God who works in you to will and to act according to His good purpose." (Philippians 2:13, NIV)

Give the **"Zipper Illustration."** (See page 203, #18)

ILLUSTRATION: _____ Zipper Illustration _____.

"If anyone does not have the Spirit of Christ, he does not belong to Christ." (Romans 8:9b, NIV)

> "What distinguishes a Christian from a non-Christian?"

A. The Holy Spirit ____ indwells ____ all genuine believers.

> Move through the following verses and blanks, reading and discussing as you go. This lesson should be an exciting new step of growth and encouragement for your Timothy.

"Because you are sons, God sent the Spirit of His Son into our hearts, the Spirit who calls out, 'Abba, Father.'" (Galatians 4:6, NIV)

"Guard the good deposit that was entrusted to you – guard it with the help of the Holy Spirit who lives in us." (2 Timothy 1:14, NIV)

> "Isn't it wonderful that God has made provision for us to succeed in the Christian life by giving us the Holy Spirit?"

B. The Holy Spirit is active in the entire salvation process.

1. He ____ convicts ____ the world of sin.

   "And He, when He comes, will convict the world concerning sin, and righteousness, and judgment." (John 16:8)

2. He ____ glorifies ____ Christ.

   "When the Counselor comes, whom I will send to you from the Father, the Spirit of truth who goes out from the Father, He will testify about Me." (John 15:26, NIV)

   "He shall glorify Me; for He shall take of Mine, and shall disclose it to you." (John 16:14)

3. He uses the ____ Word of God ____ as a sword.

"And take the helmet of salvation, and the sword of the Spirit, which is the word of God." (Ephesians 6:17)

4. He ___draws___ people to the truth.

"And the Spirit and the bride say, 'Come.' And let the one who hears say, 'Come.' And let the one who is thirsty come; let the one who wishes take the water of life without cost." (Revelation 22:17)

"You men who are stiff-necked and uncircumcised in heart and ears are always resisting the Holy Spirit; you are doing just as your fathers did." (Acts 7:51)

5. He ___frees___ us from the bondage of legalism so we can enjoy the grace of God.

"Now the Lord is the Spirit; and where the Spirit of the Lord is, there is liberty." (2 Corinthians 3:17)

"But if you are led by the Spirit, you are not under the Law." (Galatians 5:18)

6. He ___washes___ us, and enables us to become born-again followers of Christ.

"But when the kindness and love of God our Savior appeared, He saved us, not because of righteous things we had done, but because of His mercy. He saved us through the washing of rebirth and renewal by the Holy Spirit, whom He poured out on us generously through Jesus Christ our Savior." (Titus 3:4-6, NIV)

7. He comes to ___dwell in us___ at the moment of our salvation.

"Peter replied, 'Repent and be baptized, every one of you, in the name of Jesus Christ for the forgiveness of your sins. And you will receive the gift of the Holy Spirit.'" (Acts 2:38, NIV)

8. He ___insures___ our future with Christ in heaven!

"In Him, you also, after listening to the message of truth, the gospel of your salvation – having also believed, you were sealed in Him with the Holy Spirit of promise, who is given as a pledge of our inheritance, with a view to the redemption of God's own possession, to the praise of His glory." (Ephesians 1:13 & 14)

9. He gives us ___assurance___ of salvation.

"The Spirit Himself bears witness with our spirit that we are children of God." (Romans 8:16)

"By this we know that we abide in Him and He in us, because He has given us of His Spirit." (1 John 4:13)

C. The Holy Spirit empowers us to ___witness___ with boldness!

"But you shall receive power when the Holy Spirit has come upon you; and you shall be My witnesses both in Jerusalem, and in all Judea and Samaria, and even to the remotest part of the earth." (Acts 1:8)

D. The Holy Spirit is our ___helper___.

"But I tell you the truth, it is to your advantage that I go away; for if I do not go away, the Helper shall not come to you; but if I go, I will send Him to you." (John 16:7)

Give the **"Lawnmower Illustration."** (See page 204, #19)

ILLUSTRATION: ___Lawnmower___.

E. The Holy Spirit empowers us to develop a godly character.

1. He transforms us into the ___Lord's likeness___.

"And we . . . are being transformed into His likeness with ever-increasing glory, which comes from the Lord, who is the Spirit." (2 Corinthians 3:18, NIV)

2. He empowers us to exemplify godly ___character___ qualities and ___attitudes___.

"But the fruit of the Spirit is love, joy, peace, patience, kindness, goodness, faithfulness, gentleness, self-control; against such things there is no law." (Galatians 5:22 & 23)

3. He gives us ___strength___.

"I pray that out of His glorious riches He may strengthen you with power through His Spirit . . ." (Ephesians 3:16, NIV)

4. He enables us to overflow with ___hope___ !

"May the God of hope fill you with all joy and peace as you trust in Him, so that you may overflow with hope by the power of the Holy Spirit." (Romans 15:13, NIV)

5. He fills us with ___joy___ !

"And the disciples were continually filled with joy and with the Holy Spirit." (Acts 13:52)

F. The Holy Spirit helps us ___overcome temptation___.

"But I say, walk by the Spirit, and you will not carry out the desire of the flesh." (Galatians 5:16)

"Those who live according to the sinful nature have their minds set on what that nature desires; but those who live in accordance with the Spirit have their minds set on what the Spirit desires. The mind of sinful man is death, but the mind controlled by the Spirit is life and peace." (Romans 8:5 & 6, NIV)

G. The Holy Spirit _____teaches_____ us.

"But the Counselor, the Holy Spirit, whom the Father will send in My name, will teach you all things." (John 14:26a, NIV)

"We have not received the spirit of the world but the Spirit who is from God, that we may understand what God has freely given us." (1 Corinthians 2:12, NIV)

H. The Holy Spirit _____directs_____ us where and how to share our Christian witness.

> "Philip was told to witness to an Ethiopian eunuch."

"The Spirit told Philip, 'Go to that chariot and stay near it.' Then Philip ran up to the chariot and heard the man reading Isaiah the prophet. 'Do you understand what you are reading?' Philip asked. 'How can I,' he said, 'unless someone explains it to me?' So he invited Philip to come up and sit with him." (Acts 8:29-31, NIV)

> "Paul was not allowed to witness in Bithynia."

"Paul and his companions traveled throughout the region of Phrygia and Galatia, having been kept by the Holy Spirit from preaching the word in the province of Asia. When they came to the border of Mysia, they tried to enter Bithynia, but the Spirit of Jesus would not allow them to." (Acts 16:6 & 7, NIV)

> "Peter was led by the Spirit to share the Gospel with Cornelius."

"The Spirit told me to have no hesitation about going with them. These six brothers also went with me, and we entered the man's house." (Acts 11:12, NIV)

I. The Holy Spirit helps us receive _____God's love_____ into our hearts.

"And hope does not disappoint us, because God has poured out His love into our hearts by the Holy Spirit, whom He has given us." (Romans 5:5, NIV)

J. The Holy Spirit ____sanctifies____ us.

"Sanctify means to cleanse, purify, and set apart for special use."

"Who have been chosen according to the foreknowledge of God the Father, through the sanctifying work of the Spirit, for obedience to Jesus Christ and sprinkling by His blood." (1 Peter 1:2, NIV)

K. The Holy Spirit ___unites___ us and baptizes us into one body.

"For by one Spirit we were all baptized into one body, whether Jews or Greeks, whether slaves or free, and we were all made to drink of one Spirit." (1 Corinthians 12:13)

L. The Holy Spirit compassionately ____intercedes____ for us as we pray.

"In the same way, the Spirit helps us in our weakness. We do not know what we ought to pray for, but the Spirit Himself intercedes for us with groans that words cannot express. And He who searches our hearts knows the mind of the Spirit, because the Spirit intercedes for the saints in accordance with God's will." (Romans 8:26 & 27, NIV)

M. The Holy Spirit empowers us to ____confront____ false teachers.

"Then Saul, who was also called Paul, filled with the Holy Spirit, looked straight at Elymas and said, 'You are a child of the devil and an enemy of everything that is right! You are full of all kinds of deceit and trickery. Will you never stop perverting the right ways of the Lord?'" (Acts 13:9 & 10, NIV)

N. The Holy Spirit is actively involved in the __resurrection__ of all believers.

"And if the Spirit of Him who raised Jesus from the dead is living in you, He who raised Christ from the dead will also give life to your mortal bodies through His Spirit, who lives in you." (Romans 8:11, NIV)

O. The Holy Spirit empowers Christians to carry out certain ministries for the common good.

These ministries are called _____spiritual gifts_____ .
They are listed in Romans Chapter 12, 1 Corinthians Chapter 12, and Ephesians Chapter 4. Every Christian has at least one of these gifts.

"Now to each one the manifestation of the Spirit is given for the common good." (1 Corinthians 12:7, NIV)

P. The Holy Spirit _____fills us_____ .

"And do not get drunk with wine, for that is dissipation, but be filled with the Spirit." (Ephesians 5:18)

> "What two commands are given in this verse?"

God's way of empowering you to live a victorious Christian life is by filling you with the Holy Spirit, moment-by-moment. You will be filled with (directed and empowered by) the Holy Spirit as you:

1. Live by faith.

    "And without faith it is impossible to please Him." (Hebrews 11:6a)

2. Confess and turn away from all known sin.

"If we confess our sins, He is faithful and righteous to forgive us our sins and to cleanse us from all unrighteousness." (1 John 1:9)

3. Consciously yield each area of your life to God's control.

"For all who are being led by the Spirit of God, these are sons of God." (Romans 8:14)

Give the **"Sponge"** illustration. (See page 205, #20)

ILLUSTRATION:_____Sponge_____.

1. After you present the "Sponge" illustration, Ask your Timothy if he wants God to fill and control his life.
2. Lead your Timothy in a time of silent prayer, confessing all sins. Mention the fact that we need to be clean, usable vessels for His use.
3. Next, pray together in faith and yield all areas of your lives to God. Ask God to fill you with His Spirit and control the following specific areas. Mention each area verbally, pausing for a moment of silent prayer before moving to the next one.
   - Thought life
   - Time
   - Personal Discipline
   - Ethics
   - Money
   - Relationships
4. Thank God for His forgiveness, cleansing, and filling. This should be one of your greatest times of study, prayer, and commitment together!

_____

_____

_____

_____

_____

TIMOTHY'S WEEKLY SPIRITUAL GROWTH ASSIGNMENT:

A. Continue your daily Quiet Times using your *Spiritual Journal* and the Quiet Time Reading Guide. Be prepared to share your insights next week.

B. Take sermon notes using your *Spiritual Journal*. Be prepared to share your highlights next week.

C. Continue reading the Gospel of John at your own pace.

DISCIPLER'S WEEKLY SPIRITUAL GROWTH ASSIGNMENT:

Read Chapter 11, "Discipleship As A Lifestyle," starting on page 185.

SESSION SEVEN DISCIPLER'S DISCUSSION GUIDE

7

DISCUSS LAST WEEK'S ASSIGNMENTS

1. Ask him to share his Scriptural insights, prayers, and applications from each Quiet Time this past week.
2. Share one of your Quiet Times.
3. Exchange highlights from your sermon notes.
4. During this last session, be *praying* about continuing together using *A Call To Growth*. Remember that your goal is spiritual reproduction. This is why the next step is so important in terms of the Great Commission.

_____

_____

_____

_____

BUILDING A CHRISTIAN CHARACTER

---

1. "Scripture memory helps us grow in Christ's likeness."
2. "The Psalmist said, *'Thy Word I have treasured in my heart that I may not sin against Thee.'*" (Psalm 119:11)

_____

_____

The more Scripture we treasure in our hearts, the easier it is for the Holy Spirit to *guide* and *protect* us.

A. Scripture Memory helps us resist _____ temptation _____
   and live in _____ purity _____.

"How can a young man keep his way pure? By keeping it according to Thy word." (Psalm 119:9)

---

1. "Purity is a daily decision that has never been easy."
2. "Have you set any standards regarding the kinds of movies and television shows you watch? How about the kinds of books and magazines that you read?"
3. "A recent study found that 94% of all pregnancies on North American soap operas were illegitimate. This is indicative of the downward moral trend in public entertainment that affects every one of us."

_____

_____

If you fill your _____ mind _____ with sinful thoughts, they will eventually influence your _____ actions _____.

"What do you think this verse means?
'*...as he thinks in his heart, so is he.'*" (Proverbs 23:7a, NKJV)

_____

_____

> "Explain the following quote."

"If you sow a *thought*, you will reap an *action*; if you sow an action, you will reap a *habit;* if you sow a habit, you will reap a *character;* and if you sow a character, you will reap a *life.*"

> Give the **"Indian Chief"** illustration. (See page 206, #21)

ILLUSTRATION: _____ the Indian Chief _____ .

"Above all else, guard your heart, for it is the wellspring of life." (Proverbs 4:23, NIV)

> 1. "How can we practically apply this instruction?"
> 2. Share a recent victory in your own thought life. (Be real and remember to keep the emphasis on the *victory* rather than the problem.)
> 3. Give the **"Black Ink"** illustration. (See page 206, #22)

ILLUSTRATION: _____ Black Ink _____ .

B. Knowing the truth reminds us of the ___ consequences ___ **of sin**.

"Be not deceived; God is not mocked: for whatsoever a man soweth, that shall he also reap." (Galatians 6:7, KJV)

> 1. "Satan never talks about the *consequences* of sin, but the Bible does! Paul describes the certainty of judgement which will come to every person who persists in living a sinful life."
> 2. Briefly recount a personal experience or real life illustration which demonstrates the high *cost* of sin.
> 3. "Being tempted is not a sin, but giving into temptation is."

"But put on the Lord Jesus Christ, and make no provision for the flesh." (Romans 13:14, NKJV)

"I would like to share an illustration that underscores the *faithfulness* of God and the value of Scripture memory in the times of temptation."
Give the **"Charles Swindoll"** illustration. (See page 206, #23)

ILLUSTRATION: _____ Charles Swindoll _____.

C. Scripture Memory channels your thoughts in a positive direction.

"Finally, brethren, whatever is true, whatever is honorable, whatever is right, whatever is pure, whatever is lovely, whatever is of good repute, if there is any excellence and if anything worthy of praise, let your mind dwell on these things." (Philippians 4:8)

"Can you see how memorizing a verse like this can help you resist temptation?"

_____

_____

**D. Scripture Memory provides help when you____ need ____
        it most ____ !**

"In the wilderness, the Lord relied on memorized portions of the Old Testament to help Him resist the temptations of Satan. When He was tempted to turn stones into bread, He responded. . ."
(Read the next verse.)

_____

_____

"Man shall not live by bread alone, but by every word that proceedeth out of the mouth of God." (Matthew 4:4b, KJV)

**E. Scripture Memory equips you to _____ share Christ _____
    with others.**

Peter said, *"Always be prepared to give an answer to everyone who asks you to give the reason for the hope that you have."* (1 Peter 3:15, NIV)

The writer of Hebrews said, *"For the word of God is living and active and sharper than any two-edged sword. . ."* (Hebrews 4:12a) The Word of God brings conviction of sin and the awareness of Christ to the hearts of unbelievers.

F. It provides direction for making wise daily __decisions__.

---

1. "When you make decisions based upon the Bible, you will make wise choices and enjoy a *fulfilling* life."
2. "For example, suppose you were considering a serious long-term relationship with a non-Christian. The Bible makes it clear that this would be a poor decision. The Scripture warns, *'Do not be bound together with unbelievers; for what partnership have righteousness and lawlessness, or what fellowship has light with darkness?'"* (2 Corinthians 6:14)

"Thy word is a lamp to my feet, and a light to my path." (Psalm 119:105)

We should make our decisions in light of Biblical principles.

HOW CAN I INTERNALIZE GOD'S WORD?

A. Build the Bible into __your daily thoughts__.

---

1. "A good plan is to start memorizing one verse per week."
2. "If we continue with *A Call To Growth*, you will receive 11 verses and a memory verse card holder."
3. "A Memory Packet containing 52 verses is located in the Resource Section on page 113."

B. Learn the __context__.

"Learn the Context," (See page 207, #24)

_____

_____

C. Utilize natural ____methods____.

   1. Learn phrases one at a time, adding them as you go.

1. "A practical approach is to say your memory verse during your Quiet Time and before each meal."
2. "You need to concentrate on a few words until a phrase is completely memorized."
3. "Repeat the phrase several times."
4. "Add additional phrases, one at a time, until you have memorized the complete verse or passage."

   2. Meditate on the meaning of each phrase.

D. Repeat the reference before and after each verse.

   Think of the reference as an integral part of the verse itself.

"It is usually easier to memorize a verse than to recall its reference. That's why we need to repeat the reference *before* and *after* a memory verse."

E. Review for ____effectiveness____.

   One of the easiest ways to review is to __share__ new verses with your friends *". . . iron sharpens iron."* (Proverbs 27:17b)

"Your Journal is designed to help you learn a new verse each week."
"Let's open our *Spiritual Journal*s to your current Quiet Time page and write out Psalm 119:11 in the space provided."

F. Meditate for ____fellowship____.

Filling your mind and heart with Scripture will greatly increase the quality of your fellowship with God.

David said *". . . I remember Thee on my bed. I meditate on Thee in the night. . ."* (Psalm 63:6)

"How blessed is the man who does not walk in the counsel of the wicked . . . but his delight is in the law of the Lord, and in His law he meditates day and night." (Psalm 1:1 & 2)

---

1. "Christian meditation involves prayerfully considering, reflecting, and focusing on all the aspects of a truth, then seeking to apply that truth to your life. True meditation leads to godly thoughts and actions!"
2. "Through meditation, you will experience the true delight of coming to know your heavenly Father in greater depth."

_____

_____

_____

_____

THE CHALLENGE TO BUILD A GODLY LIFE!

Paul said, *". . . discipline yourself for the purpose of godliness."* (1 Timothy 4:7b)

"Discipline is the key to a strong finish in the exciting race God has set before us. We need to pursue His will with endurance!"

_____

_____

_____

_____

"But flee from these things, you man of God; and pursue righteousness, godliness, faith, love, perseverance and gentleness." (1 Timothy 6:11)

1. "If you choose to consistently feed yourself spiritually, you will continue to grow. If you don't, you will stop growing and settle into lukewarmness and mediocrity. The Lord said, ' *I know your deeds, that you are neither cold nor hot; I would that you were cold or hot.* '" (Revelation 3:15)

_____

_____

2. Read the following verse together, and enjoy a time of personal commitment in prayer.

_____

_____

"*. . . Let us throw off everything that hinders and the sin that so easily entangles, and let us run with perseverance the race marked out for us. Let us fix our eyes on Jesus, the author and perfecter of our faith, who for the joy set before Him endured the cross, scorning its shame, and sat down at the right hand of the throne of God.*" (Hebrews 12:1 & 2, NIV)

A CALL TO FAITHFULNESS!

"*. . . If you abide in My word, then you are truly disciples of Mine.*" (John 8:31)

- Continue to enjoy daily Quiet Times using your Quiet Time Reading Guide.

- Memorize Psalm 119:11 for personal growth.

- Keep witnessing to others about Christ.

- Continue reading the Bible at your own pace.

- Enjoy journaling, worship, and prayer.

Congratulations upon completing *A Call To Joy!* We sincerely hope that you will continue the spiritual growth process so you will keep maturing in Christ!

A CALL TO GROWTH

This highly practical series includes eleven sessions teaching:

* The *five* most basic aspects of prayer.

* The "hows" and "whys" of independent Bible study.

* How to share your faith naturally using *three* different lifestyle methods:

  1. **A Word of Truth**
  2. **A Personal Testimony**
  3. **"The Bridge Illustration"**

* Principles for dealing with *temptation.*

* The joy of *giving* to the Lord with a grateful heart.

* Keys to continued personal growth.

"For I am confident of this very thing, that He who began a good work in you will perfect it until the day of Christ Jesus."
(Philippians 1:6)

INSPIRATIONAL READING

Chapters
1 – 5

CHAPTER 1

THE LOVE
OF GOD

"Yet to all who received Him, to those who believed in His name, He gave the right to become children of God." (John 1:12, NIV)

Congratulations for indicating your desire to make Jesus Christ the Lord of your life. This is the most rewarding and important decision you will ever make!

During the next few weeks, it will be my privilege to assist you as you learn how to grow in your personal relationship with God. To begin with, let's review what you did when you invited Christ to be your Savior. You may have done this recently, or at some time in the past. But you now desire to grow in spiritual maturity.

Let's start reviewing what the Scripture teaches in John 1:12. If after reading this passage you still lack assurance that you have received Christ, a prayer is provided on page 43. Praying this prayer with faith and understanding will enable you to personally settle this matter in your heart.

GOD'S LOVE

The depth of God's love for us is revealed in the fact that He wants us to become His very own children. Everyone in the world was created by God, and *each one of us shares the same heavenly invitation to become far more than His creation.* God wants us to be His children, members of His family.

To explain this invitation, the Bible focuses on two important words of action: *believe* and *receive.* Pretend you have a glass of water in your hand. You are hot, thirsty, and nearly dehydrated. You believe the water is cool and good, but it cannot quench your thirst until you drink it – until your parched body receives it. *Believing without receiving is not enough!* But believing is the beginning.

God designed our physical bodies to need water, and He uniquely created water to meet that physical need. The spiritual principle of life is exactly the same. We needed to know God, and God sent His Son, Jesus Christ, into the world to meet that spiritual need. When we receive Christ into our hearts, we come to know our heavenly Father. Through this unique relationship, He provides all the love, forgiveness, and guidance we will ever need. He quenches our thirst for His presence. His well will never run dry. Another parallel between physical reality and spiritual reality can be seen in architecture. No superstructure is ever built without first laying a foundation. This is universally true. In 1 Corinthians 3:11, Paul says, *". . .no man can lay a foundation other than the one which is laid which is Christ Jesus."* You must believe enough in the Lord's power to change you, receive Him by faith, and let Him establish that spiritual foundation in your life.

BEGINNING A NEW LIFE

Years ago, in Anchorage, Alaska, I taught these verses during a conference on spiritual growth. A young woman who had attended every session seemed to be unhappy; there was no radiance in her smile. She didn't laugh when others laughed, or take part in the activities. Toward the close of the week, as I taught on salvation, she began to cry. Soon, she made her way to the front of the auditorium. I asked if she understood what I had been saying. She said that she had not understood anything for four nights, but when John 1:12 on *believing* and *receiving* was explained, she saw her spiritual condition.

I explained that *once you realize your need for forgiveness, there are two steps to salvation. The first is intellectual acceptance. The second is your willingness to receive Christ by faith.* I said, "He is a gentleman and will not force His way into your life. He knocks and wants to come in, but you must offer the invitation." She had never understood this before.

She told me that she lived in an apartment about three blocks from the church, but had never attended services. She had been living in adultery with a man for a long time. The week before, he had left a note simply saying, "I'm leaving, you'll never see me again." At the age of 23, she had a baby but no marriage, a past but no future, a present but no happiness. She read the note and threw herself on the bed. She prayed, "O, God, I haven't talked to You for years, but if You are there, if You are real, please answer me. I have made a terrible mess of my life and I need Your help. I need forgiveness. I want to live differently."

Here was a young woman who had been to church not more than three times in her entire life. She had no relationship with God, but was now sincerely seeking Him. In the quietness of her heart, God impressed her to leave her apartment and enter the first church building she saw. He let her know that the help she needed was waiting there. By God's providence, that was where I was leading a conference on spiritual growth.

When she entered the church building, she saw books and a registration table. She paid the conference fee, thinking that must be what it cost to go to church. Because ten churches were participating in the meeting, everyone assumed that she was a member of a congregation other than their own and no one suspected her need. But she persevered and sat alone every night.

One evening, I went through the plan of salvation, illustrating how we were created by God, but had been separated from Him by sin. I explained the wonderful news: that through believing in Christ and receiving Him, one could become a child of God. As the Holy Spirit opened her eyes, for the first time in her life she saw the importance of receiving Christ.

Her new life began with a prayer like this: *"Lord, I believe in You and want You to be my Savior. Please come into my heart and take control of my life. I have sinned and need Your love and forgiveness."* Her overwhelming joy was evident as she gave thanks that her prayer had been answered. Through the Lord Jesus Christ, she was born into God's kingdom and became one of His very own children.

Today, many people do not understand that intellectual belief in God is not enough. They are surprised to learn that the Scriptures say that even the demons believe in one God, but that doesn't get them into heaven. Personal commitment is required for salvation. That is why the act of *receiving* Christ is so important.

LIVING WITH ASSURANCE

After laying the spiritual foundation of *believing* and *receiving*, what comes next? In 1 John 5:13, the Bible says, *"These things I have written to you who believe in the name of the Son of God, in order that you may know that you have eternal life."* The word *"know"* stands out as the emphasis of this verse. As His children, God wants us to be assured of His love, faithfulness, and supreme adequacy to see us through both this life and the next. In His love, He chose to let us *know* rather than guess or only hope about the reality of our salvation. God does not intend for us to wait through life to find out if we are going to heaven. First John was written so that God's children might have that certainty.

In Romans 8:16, the apostle Paul says, *"And the Spirit Himself bears witness with our spirit that we are children of God."* It is God who reminds you that you are His child. With each passing year, your assurance and understanding of that reality will grow. Though remembering the exact hour or day when you received Christ is desirable, it is not necessary. However, knowing that there was such a time is essential. Billy Graham's wife, Ruth, reared on the mission field in China, came to faith at an early age. When asked about her conversion, she once replied, "I'm not sure when the sun came up, but I'm certain that it's shining!" This certainty is the birthright of every person who receives Christ into his life.

I well remember my own conversion. I was only ten years old and alone in my room. Though I vividly recall making the decision, I cannot remember the date. But I will never forget the joy that filled my heart when I awakened my parents and said, "Mother and Dad, I have become a Christian." I knew what had happened! Although I had only prayed the single word, "yes," God knew all that it implied. In later years, I have often thought of the simple prayer of the repentant thief on the cross who said, *"Lord, remem-*

ber me when You come into Your kingdom." (Luke 23:42, NKJV) That was not a wordy request, but it was enough to make the difference for eternity, because God knew he meant it.

God looks into our hearts. What we mean by what we say is far more important to Him than the way we say it. The sincere prayer of the smallest child is as pleasing and acceptable to Him as the petition of the most mature adult. If you have the inner peace that comes from the assurance that you have already sincerely invited Christ into your heart, reading the pages that follow will significantly deepen the quality of your relationship with Him.

However, if your life still has no spiritual foundation, and you lack the assurance that you have received Christ into your life, you have *nothing to fear*. God has promised to honor the desires of your heart (Psalm 37:4 & 5). Though you may have believed in Christ with your mind, you now realize your need to personally receive Him into your life. He is prepared to answer your petition.

Prayers of sincere repentance based upon Jesus' famous parable about the prodigal son (Luke 15:11-32) have been expressed to God by millions across the centuries. Here is a prayer that includes what the Lord taught in that parable. It is called "A Prayer for Salvation." If you still feel a need to be certain of your own relationship with Christ, pray this prayer in faith.

There is no magic in the particular words of this prayer, for *receiving Christ is an act of the will. Your prayer simply reflects the inward decision you are making.* Have you trusted Christ completely for forgiveness and guidance? If not, this moment and your earnest commitment will make the difference in how and where you spend eternity.

If you have been *hoping* that you are a Christian, but want to know for *certain*, God wants you to have that *assurance*. Why not pause now and quietly talk with Him? Consider each thought in this prayer and express it to God in your own personal way.

A PRAYER FOR SALVATION

"Lord Jesus, I am a sinner. But I am sorry for my sins. I want to turn from my sins. I am willing to begin a new life with Your help. Lord Jesus, please come into my heart and life right now. From this moment forward, my life belongs to You and You alone. I will love You, serve You, tell others about You, and trust You to live Your life through me. Thank You Lord, for coming into my life and for forgiving my sins today."

What have you just done? You have received the Lord Jesus Christ as your personal Savior! Because of this, there is great joy in heaven. You might be saying to yourself, "This is wonderful! But what should I do next?" For salvation, you have made the all-important step of receiving Christ by faith. Now you must learn how to walk in Him.

CHAPTER 2

LEARNING
TO WALK

"As you therefore have received Christ Jesus the Lord, so walk in Him." (Colossians 2:6)

Learning how to walk in Christ is your next step in Christian growth. In this step, you will discover the joy of telling others about your decision to follow Christ. The Lord said, *"Whoever acknowledges Me before men, I will also acknowledge him before My Father in heaven."* (Matthew 10:32, NIV) What does that mean? Simply this: When you love someone, it is natural to talk about them. You want others to know about the close friendship you share. *The Lord wants no secret disciples, and when you love Him, you will want to be baptized, join a church fellowship, and begin to witness where you work or go to school. These things will come naturally as you grow.*

Before a person learns how to walk, he must learn to crawl. Walking and maturing are part of this process. There is no single moment when you suddenly become mature. It is the same in your spiritual pilgrimage: birth (receiving Christ) comes first. Then comes crawling, walking, and finally running. This involves wonderful years of growing in fellowship with God. The apostle Paul

45

speaks of Christian maturity as running the race and finishing the course (1 Corinthians 9:24, 2 Timothy 4:7).

Walking requires energy, and just as we gain physical strength through eating, we need to nourish ourselves spiritually as well. In 1 Peter 2:2, the apostle says, *"Like newborn babes, long for the pure milk of the word, that by it you may grow..."* When you were born, the first thing you needed was nourishment. A child needs milk. You don't have to instruct him to want it – the desire is natural. There is an excitement and beautiful satisfaction when that need is met. *On a spiritual level, the desire to know God's Word corresponds to a baby's natural hunger. For this reason, the Word of God is often referred to as spiritual food.*

How do you feed yourself spiritually as you learn to walk in Christ? God has equipped us with five senses. One of these senses is the ability to hear. The Bible says, *"Faith comes from what is preached, and what is preached comes from the word of Christ."* (Romans 10:17, JB) Every time you attend a Bible study or go to church, you have the opportunity to hear the Word of God. Each time you listen, you are given new spiritual truths. This is God's way of increasing our faith. Jesus said, *". . . Man shall not live by bread alone, but by every word that proceeds from the mouth of God."* (Matthew 4:4, NKJV) *The Bible itself is our source of spiritual nourishment.*

Listening is a primary means of spiritual growth; however, there is an unexpected hurdle which we must all overcome. *Scientists have proven that we forget approximately 90 to 95 percent of what we hear after 72 hours. If you heard your favorite preacher or could even listen to the apostle Paul, you would still forget about 90 percent of what he said after three days. The truth is, most of us cannot remember much from last Sunday's sermon. This is not because of a lack of dedication. Our problem is retention!* Unless what we hear meets a very specific need in our lives, we simply cannot remember it.

So note-taking is important. It compensates for our human tendency to forget; it encourages those who preach and teach from the Scripture, and it helps us meditate on what we hear, so we can apply God's Word in our lives.

I discovered the value of note-taking after several years of frustration. As a teenager, I publicly rededicated my life nine times. I guess the people at our church must have thought I had a lot of problems. In reality, what I was trying to say was that I wanted to grow deeper in my commitment to Christ. It was not that I had become less dedicated. I simply didn't know how to retain the blessings I was receiving. Perhaps you have had a similar experience. Unfortunately, there was no place on the commitment card which said, "I want to be a man or woman whom God can use, and I need someone to teach me."

Learning how to listen will be essential to your spiritual growth, and note-taking will help you succeed. Most teachers have the tendency to slow down, make their points clearer, and even repeat them when they see someone is taking notes.

WHERE TO TAKE SERMON NOTES

It is appropriate to take notes on God's Word at every opportunity. However, even this small discipline requires a little planning. Taking notes on scraps of paper, bulletin inserts, and offering envelopes will not result in the kind of growth which you are seeking. For this reason, the *Spiritual Journal* with a helpful note-taking section has been developed.

The use of this Journal will help keep you from the experience of my good friend, a West Texas cattleman, who was at a Bible conference in Houston. A wonderful British Bible teacher was exhorting us from the Scriptures. As we walked across the street together, I asked him, "How is God speaking to you through this conference?" This man, who was in his seventies and wore a Stetson hat, cowboy boots, and a western suit, said, "Son, my cup is full and running over." That was his explanation of how greatly he was being blessed. About six weeks later, I ran into him in another city. When I asked, "How is your cup?" he pensively replied, "Had a hole in it."

Perhaps you have had the same experience. You went to a conference, church service, or a crusade, and you were greatly blessed, only to discover a few days later that you felt empty again. Remember, your problem may not be a lack of dedication, but simply a lack of retention.

WHY TAKE SERMON NOTES?

Some Christians live the first year of their Christian lives over many times. Instead of growing, they end up on a treadmill, learning and forgetting the same lessons year after year. The object of spiritual growth is not to live the first year nine times, but to live nine progressive years of the Christian life!

According to a national survey, the average minister spends twenty hours per week in sermon preparation. When he realizes that Sunday after Sunday, his average church member will retain only three minutes of content from a thirty-minute sermon, it has to be discouraging. If you want to encourage your pastor, let him know that you are serious about listening. When you meet him at the door instead of saying, "I enjoyed the service," mention one specific verse, insight, or illustration that helped you. Tell him how God used the sermon to positively affect your life. Through this, he will know that you heard what the Holy Spirit was saying through the message.

Practical application is retention's best friend. When your actions and attitudes are positively affected, your recall will increase as well. Science has demonstrated that you remember 90 percent of what you hear, read, and then do. Your spiritual objective should therefore focus on James 1:22 (NIV), which says, *"Do not merely listen to the word, and so deceive yourselves. Do what it says."* Your first practical step toward victory is simply beginning a lifestyle of taking good notes.

The objective of note-taking is not to outline the sermon or the Bible study lesson. What matters is recording what the Holy Spirit is teaching you personally as you listen to the Word of God. Write down the things that will make a difference in your life, insights you can actually apply. The test of good listening and good application is life itself. When you leave church or a Bible study, you need to go out better prepared to live positively and effectively.

REVERENCE FOR SCRIPTURE

Spiritual growth occurs when we meditate upon what God says and then apply it in our daily lives. Because this is true, we need to cultivate an attitude like the people of Ezra's day. They hungered for a Word from God! Nehemiah 8:2-6 says: *"And Ezra, the priest, brought the Law before the congregation, and he read therein from morning until mid-day, and the ears of the people were attentive. And when he read, all the people stood up, and Ezra blessed the Lord, the great God, and all the people answered, 'Amen, Amen.'"* (Paraphrased)

Why did they stand up? Wouldn't they have been more comfortable sitting down? Yes. But they stood up out of respect for God's Word. Can you imagine such a congregation? Can you believe that they chose to stand up all that time?

Today, it's hard to get people to come to listen, even in air-conditioned comfort. But to Ezra's congregation, inconvenience didn't matter.

"When Ezra read, all the people stood up. . ." These words took on a fresh meaning for me several years ago. I was once in an African congregation that stood every time the Bible was read. The respect that the congregation held for the Scriptures convinced me that too many of us do not value the sacredness of God's Word.

In recent years, some countries have been blessed with an amazing array of up-to-date translations which include a wide assortment of chain references, concordances, and other helpful information. *With all these modern blessings, you must carefully guard against taking your Bible for granted. The privilege of reading its sacred pages is still beyond the reach of a large percentage of the world's population.* Only in the light of this overwhelming truth can we begin to appreciate the value of its availability.

The scarcity of Bibles in other countries was vividly brought to my attention several years ago as counselors were being trained for an evangelistic campaign in a West African country. Although Christians had been in the area for decades, the nation was largely made up of animists (those who still hold ancient pagan beliefs about multiple gods and spirits, usually active in nature). Being unfamiliar with many of their country's unique problems, I wrote ahead to organize the crusade in a routine manner. Our standard Bible study requirements caused the counselors in training to walk for miles, sometimes barefooted, to join a friend who owned a prized possession – a Bible. Months later, when I arrived to preach, my heart was deeply moved when I realized how insensitive we had been due to our Western assumption that every Christian had a Bible.

In Ezra's day, the problem was even more pronounced. People had to gather to hear and listen to God's Word from the handwritten scrolls which had been painstakingly copied.

CARRYING YOUR BIBLE

Owning a Bible is a privilege, and carrying it with you is a witness in itself. Spurgeon, a famous British Christian, used to say, "Carry your Bible with you every place you go, because it will preach a thousand sermons a day!" How true this is. When people see your Bible, they automatically think of its message; and the Holy Spirit will apply conviction, comfort, or hope to their hearts.

As a student, I learned this valuable lesson. One day in class, my Bible toppled off my other books and landed on the floor. My agnostic teacher immediately stopped the class, saying, "Billie, your Bible has fallen on the floor." Though she had never received Christ as her Savior, her deep respect for what He stood for caused her to spontaneously honor His words of truth. This simple occurrence provided a natural opportunity for me to talk with her privately. I explained that if the Bible were already meaningful to her, its inspired message would affect her even more when she came to know its Author. Though she was much older and also my teacher, it was obvious from the look in her eyes that she received that suggestion with genuine appreciation.

A GODLY ATTITUDE

You will increase your joy in reading the Bible and hearing its message preached and taught if you learn an important secret.

In Memphis, Tennessee, I have a friend who was invited to be a guest speaker in a church which is known for its long services. After an hour of congregational singing and testimonies, a beautiful piano solo was played. A lady stood up in the back of the congregation and reverently said, "Yes, Lord, yes." Time passed, and another person stood and said the same thing. After several minutes, a large percentage of the congregation had stood to their feet and said, "Yes, Lord, yes."

My friend was perplexed because he had not heard a question. Finally his host, a well-known pastor looked heavenward and said, "Father, we have given You our response in advance. Now speak to us through Your messenger and tell us what it is You desire for us to do." *The secret to joy and worship is listening with a prepared heart. What God is looking for in every Christian's attitude is faith expressed in a pre-determined will to obey.*

Have you ever attended a church service when the last thing you felt like doing was worshiping the Lord? We need to guard our frame of mind and worship with a spirit of expectancy. This requires planning ahead, because invariably the whole world seems to clamor for our attention immediately prior to the worship service. What a difference it will make in your life when you come to church saying, "Yes, Lord, yes." When this is the attitude of your heart, God will begin to use your life in wonderful new ways!

Too many of us listen to God's Word as if we were partaking of a smorgasbord. We want to select a little bit of this and a little bit of that from the Bible, but we do not come with a pre-determined will to receive whatever God says we need and then apply it in our lives. All too often, our attitude is something like this: "Lord, I want to hear what You have to say to me as long as it fits what I already plan to do." The net result is that we ask Him to bless what we want to be blessed. We try to ignore what we do not want to hear. Mature worship is putting ourselves under the authority of Jesus Christ by saying, "Yes, Lord, yes. I'm available; I'm willing; I'm eager to do what You want me to do."

Having believed in Christ and having received Him as your Savior, your love for Him will be evidenced by listening to His Word and walking in obedience to His will. *Because He came to give you an abundant life, His leadership will always direct you to the highest plain of fulfillment.* We have His unfailing promise: *"I will instruct you and teach you in the way which you should go; I will counsel you with My eye upon you."* (Psalm 32:8)

Using the note-taking section of the *Spiritual Journal*, will you commit yourself to the Lord to grow in your faith by taking notes on what you hear from the Bible?

_____ Yes
_____ No

"Faith comes from what is preached, and what is preached comes from the word of Christ." (Romans 10:17, JB)

CHAPTER 3

THE PERFECT EXAMPLE

"Very early in the morning, while it was still dark, Jesus got up, left the house and went off to a solitary place, where He prayed." (Mark 1:35, NIV)

The Lord's perfect life is an example for all mankind to follow. The world has had many teachers, but only one Christ – His actions were as inspired as the words which He spoke.

THE EXAMPLE OF JESUS

He started His day with the Father, not only because He wanted to, but because in His humanity He actually needed to. Each time He departed for a season alone in prayer and personal fellowship with the Father, His human needs were met. Beyond that, He was showing His disciples how to live victoriously. He arose early on this particular morning (Mark 1:35) and chose to be totally alone. On the day before, He had preached in Capernaum, freed a man possessed by demons, healed Peter's mother-in-law, and preached again to a huge crowd where great numbers of spiritually, physically, and emotionally sick people were healed (Mark 1:21-34). It is an understatement to say that His schedule had been busy.

Everyone wanted to be with Him – the sick and disturbed, new followers, disciples in training, and hangers-on; they were all pressing in upon Him. To get any time alone with the Father, Jesus literally had to get up while it was still dark and slip away while the others were sleeping.

This devotional practice was essential in the Lord's earthly life because He lived in dependence upon the spiritual strength given to Him by His Father. He carefully reminded His disciples that no work He did was of Himself, and that no word He ever spoke was His own. He credited the Father with everything accomplished in His ministry (John 14:10). He literally lived each moment in dependence upon His Father. Ironically, our Savior who spoke only of dependence, was seen by the Jewish leaders of the day as the most independent man they had ever met (Mark 1:27).

During the Lord's solitary times of prayer, He was sometimes interrupted. Such was the case on this particular morning; *"And Simon and his companions hunted for Him; and they found Him, and said to Him, 'Everyone is looking for You.'"* (Mark 1:36 & 37) Several important lessons can be seen in this experience, but first concentrate on the person of Christ. What really happened when He was interrupted? Visualize the Lord talking to His Father. Consider the fact that He was filled with the Holy Spirit without measure (John 3:34). Allow the exalted meaning of this verse to permeate your mind; *"For in Him* (Christ) *all the fulness of Deity dwells in bodily form."* (Colossians 2:9) Everything that God is, was present in the life of Christ. Since prayer is a conversation, one could accurately say that Peter and the other apostles unknowingly interrupted a holy time of communion among God the Father, God the Son, and God the Holy Spirit. To be sure, this was a most holy moment.

When the Lord's prayer time was interrupted, He demonstrated what our reaction should be. He did not chide those who intruded upon His time with the Father. He did not allow the interruption to upset His spirit or ruin His day.

His lifestyle remained consistent yet flexible, regardless of the outward circumstances. But how does this relate to us today?

PRACTICAL DEVOTIONS

The Lord Jesus and the early Christians lived in that pre-electric era when people normally went to bed early and got up early. If they wanted to do anything at night, they had to build a fire or use a small oil-burning lantern. Although Jesus rose early, it was probably after getting a good night's rest. *The point of this passage is not to rise before the sun comes up, but rather to start your day with God whenever your day normally begins.* This principle will hold true for shift workers, night watchmen, and people of every vocation.

No specific hour is established in the Bible for your daily Quiet Time. You do not have to be like the famous British cricketer, C. T. Studd, who is said to have read the Bible by candlelight in the early morning hours. I will never forget the guilt trip I went on once after hearing a marvelous sermon on the Quiet Time. After that service, I thought the only way to be spiritual was to get up at 4:00 a.m. and read the Bible by candlelight! *The key to spiritual growth is not how early, but how expectantly and consistently one meets with the Father.*

Medical science has discovered that all of us have a biological clock. Our bodies actually require differing amounts of sleep in order to work at peak efficiency. I have a good friend from Africa who only needs four or five hours of sleep per night, but most people need seven or eight.

Alexander the Great had a very unusual biological clock. It is said that when needed, he could sleep 72 hours and work 72 hours. This was one of the ways he won his battles. He wore out one army after another! No one else could concentrate on the fight that long. He learned to use his strengths and limitations, and when he died at the age of 32, he had already accomplished a great deal. It is important to get to know your own sleep requirements, so you can plan ahead to be wide awake for your Quiet Times. Eventually in your Christian experience, no matter how dedicated you are, you will face the reality of fatigue. The Lord faced it. One afternoon He went to sleep in a boat (Matthew 8:23-27) and demonstrated to His disciples that when exhausted, the most spiritual thing you can do is rest!

Relating this principle to your own Quiet Time, remember that trying to keep one eye open while reading the Bible is like attempting to talk to someone when you are only half awake. Under normal circumstances, if a person who really loves you sees that you are exhausted, he will want you to go ahead and sleep. God's attitude is clearly revealed in the Scripture when He says, *"He gives His beloved sleep."* (Psalm 127:2b, NKJV)

GETTING STARTED

Let me challenge you to join the countless millions whose lives have been changed by beginning their day with a Quiet Time. Ten to fifteen minutes each morning will make an amazing difference in your day. Why not stop right now and dedicate these "special minutes" to God. Give Him the beginnings of all your future days. Ask Him to continually remind you of the important commitment you are making. As you pray, thank Him for the high privilege of spending time alone in His presence.

All spiritual growth is based upon decisions. The choice you are making to begin a daily Quiet Time is one you will never regret. Through it, you will grow in fellowship with God and in your ability to minister to your fellow man.

Every journey starts with a first step, and a Quiet Time begins by simply waking up and getting out of bed in the morning! I am reminded of the story about a man who always stayed in bed while trying to read the Bible. One day he confessed that "Something came up," and he missed his Quiet Time. His confession was overheard by his guardian angel who candidly remarked, "Something came up, indeed! It was big and white, and looked exactly like a sheet!"

The opposite side of fatigue is oversleeping. Some people are "spendaholics." They spend God's money on this, that, and the other, and then they have nothing left to give. Others are "workaholics." They work, work, work, until no time is left to be with God because they have substituted activity for worship.

Then there is the "sleepaholic." If you are a sleepaholic, let me suggest that you memorize Proverbs 6:9, which says, *"How long will you lie down, O sluggard? When will you arise from your sleep?"* When you commit that verse to memory, the Holy Spirit will use it time after time to awaken you when you are rolling from one side of your bed to the other in the morning. I can assure you this is true, because He has used this verse with me on more than one occasion.

"I overslept" is perhaps the most commonly used excuse for not having a Quiet Time. Over the years, as I have taught on this

subject, approximately 15 percent of the conferees have said that they are very sluggish in the mornings, 15 percent have said they wake up bright and eager to begin the day. Another 70 percent say they get up reasonably well, but they still have trouble being alert. A Quiet Time is intended to be *fun*, so let me give you a few practical suggestions on this matter of being awake and alert. While some of these suggestions are more serious than others, all of them can be helpful.

Analyze what gets you awake in the morning. For my wife, it is coffee. She frequently drinks it before or during her Quiet Time. For men, let me recommend Mennen's Skin Bracer. Don't drink it – just splash it on your face, neck, elbows, and kneecaps, and you will feel like running around the room. It's tremendous! For the same effect, ladies can use Charles of the Ritz Tingling Astringent.

Exercise is also good. Recently in Korea, a veteran missionary showed me his tried and proven method. He shakes his hands vigorously while running in place for one thousand steps. This is followed by an ice cold shower! In favorable climates, a brisk morning walk before Bible reading will accomplish the same objective. The Scripture says, *"discipline yourself for the purpose of godliness"* (1 Timothy 4:7b), so whatever approach you use, make up your mind in advance to carry it through.

For those who have a particular aversion to mid-winter devotions, I have heard of one unique wake-up approach. If you sleep on the right-hand side of the bed, put your right leg out of the covers first. If you do not get up immediately, just let it hang off the edge of the bed and it will grow uncomfortable after a while. Soon you will swing your left leg over to join it. Before you know it, you will be up washing your face and getting ready for the day!

Remember this thought: even though the Scripture says, *"Be still, and know that I am God"* (Psalm 46:10a, KJV), let me suggest that you not be too still. The objective is to get out of bed to read and pray. If you do not, your Quiet Time will inevitably be too quiet!

EVENING DEVOTIONS

There are several hazards in having your devotions at night. I am not saying that God will not bless it, but it often amounts to giving Him the "leftovers" of your day. You are already tired. You have given your best to the world, your job, and the people around you. But the One who deserves the most receives the least. Make note of four hazards related to having your devotions at night: energy spent, pillow soft, lights dim, print small! I have experienced every one of these hazards and have unintentionally fallen off to sleep.

As a young Christian, I attempted to have my Quiet Time at night simply because I didn't know any better. Like so many people, I would sleep until the last minute and rush to class in the mornings. For years, my only Scripture reading and prayer was at night. My grandmother had given me a large Bible. One evening as I was reading it, the pillow seemed so soft and the light looked so dim that I soon fell asleep with the Bible on my chest. I didn't move until the next morning. While the Bible was on my chest, in the zone between sleep and wakefulness, I kept subconsciously thinking, "Something is wrong!" The Bible's weight produced a strange feeling. I remember opening my eyes very slowly and seeing the words "Holy Bible" upside down. A sentimental feeling swept over me: "I slept all night with a Bible on my chest!" There's one thing you can be sure of – that's not the way to increase your spirituality!

Charlie Riggs of the Billy Graham team has said, "The Word of God has to get into your mind, and then make an 18-inch trip down into your heart." How true that is. *You have to be alert enough to think through what you are reading if it is going to affect the way you live.*

When I heard about the value of having a Quiet Time, I accepted a six-week challenge to begin spending ten minutes each morning with God. It was like eating honey – once you taste it, you want more. The Psalmist said, *"How sweet are Thy words to my taste! Yes, sweeter than honey to my mouth!"* (Psalm 119:103) As time passed, I came to understand the testimony of Jeremiah: *"...Thy words became for me a joy and the delight of my heart..."* (Jeremiah 15:16)

You can begin your day with God and end it with Him as well. If you want to read and pray at night, that's great, as long as it is not your only Quiet Time. Enjoy your spiritual cake in the morning, and the icing before you go to sleep at night!

CHAPTER 4

THE SECRET OF GODLINESS

"Discipline yourself for the purpose of godliness." (1 Timothy 4:7b)

No one reaches godliness by accident. It is only as you seek personal purity, determine to be holy, and allow Christ to be in control that the victorious Christian life becomes experientially yours. Spiritual growth, unlike physical growth, is the product of personal commitment. We decide to discipline ourselves for the "purpose of godliness." As we make Christ-honoring decisions, He gives us all the power we need to live them out.

This new life is one which the secular world cannot fully understand. Paul describes its uniqueness in 2 Corinthians 5:17, *"Therefore if any man is in Christ, he is a new creature; the old things passed away; behold, new things have come."* Paul's personal testimony reflects his complete change in values. *"Whatever things were gain to me, those I have counted as loss. . ."* But why? *". . . In view of the surpassing value of knowing Christ Jesus my Lord. . ."* (Philippians 3:7 & 8a) *Christians have a new and different mindset.* The Scripture says, *"If you have been raised up with*

Christ, . . . Set your mind on the things above, not on the things that are on earth." (Colossians 3:1a, 2)

The new thoughts, actions, and deep affections that come with receiving Christ are nurtured by our close fellowship with Him. Like most new disciples, the first verse I ever learned was John 3:16, *"For God so loved the world, that He gave His only begotten Son, that whoever believes in Him should not perish, but have eternal life."* Years later, a friend showed me 1 Corinthians 1:9 and explained its wonderful meaning. It became my second memory verse: *"God is utterly dependable, and it is He who has called you into fellowship with His Son Jesus Christ, our Lord."* (PH) It was through this passage I discovered that every Christian has a calling – yes, a high calling to have fellowship with Christ.

GOD DESIRES OUR FELLOWSHIP

Why set aside a Quiet Time for prayer and daily Bible reading? Because God Himself is faithfully calling us into a life of fellowship with His Son. To disappoint that holy desire on the part of God for even one day would be a tragedy. In John 4:23, His desire for fellowship is emphasized by Jesus: *"An hour is coming. . .when the true worshipers shall worship the Father in spirit and truth; for such people the Father seeks to be His worshipers."* Fellowship, our highest calling, is at the very heart of our worship and everything else we do as God's children. Through it, we are participants in His highest purpose for life.

The daily Quiet Time is not a program designed by men, nor is it a legalistic ritual based on tradition. It is the outward response of our innate desire to truly know God. Listen to the words of the apostle Paul after having been a Christian for many years. The hunger of his heart was to deepen that fellowship: *"That I may know Him, and the power of His resurrection, and the fellowship of His sufferings. . ."* (Philippians 3:10a) Paul wanted to know every aspect of having a close relationship with his Creator.

Love is like that. Married couples will quickly testify that after having known and loved each other for years, they are still learning to appreciate new aspects of one another's personalities. Love is spelled T-I-M-E. To really know someone requires years of fellowship in a wide variety of circumstances. This same rule applies to your walk with God.

THE REASSURANCE OF HIS LOVE

Hunger for God is as old as man himself, but few have expressed this longing with the clarity of Moses. In his beautiful prayer he says, *"O satisfy us in the morning with Thy steadfast love that we may rejoice and be glad all of our days."* (Psalm 90:14, Paraphrased) He grasped an essential truth about God's love: It is steadfast, unchanging, and secure.

Morning by morning Moses had experienced the secret of joy and gladness. He was walking in close fellowship with the God he loved in spite of all the difficulties the world could hurl in his direction. Put yourself in his place: at the age of 80, he was responsible for moving 600,000 men and their families to the country of Canaan (Exodus 12:37). The hostile Egyptian army was behind him, a burning desert lay in front of him, and he had very little food and water. Humanly speaking, he had nothing but problems. In addition to all these obstacles, the people were unhappy most of the time. He bore the heaviest kind of responsibility in the worst kind of working environment. It was in this setting that he learned the supreme value of spending his mornings with God.

Wouldn't you like to be inwardly satisfied at the dawning of each new day? Think about a delicious meal that satisfies your hunger, or a drink that satisfies your thirst. *The daily Quiet Time is designed to satisfy your hunger for God Himself.* If you have responsibilities, live in a challenging environment, or need to be reminded that God loves you, the same joy that Moses experienced is ready and available.

If Christians cannot live as proof of an abundant, positive joy, who in this world can? The person in your mirror has a right to be happy! You have been redeemed and are now God's child. You are free to live out your potential to the fullest extent. Ephesians 2:10 says, *"For we are His workmanship, created in Christ Jesus for good works, which God prepared beforehand, that we should walk in them."* You are a special person with a special mission. Each and every morning, God wants to remind you of who you are in Christ.

OUR NEED FOR DIRECTION

Psalm 143:8 is one of many practical verses in the Bible. It deals specifically with having a daily Quiet Time. David says, *"Cause me to hear Thy lovingkindness in the morning, for in Thee do I trust: cause me to know the way wherein I should walk; for I lift up my soul unto Thee."* (KJV) If there was ever a man in the Bible who needed to have a daily Quiet Time for guidance, it was David. When he says, *"I lift up my soul unto Thee,"* it literally means, "I place my life in Your hands."

Consider David, a man whose life was lived in constant conflict – a man's man, fearless and decisive. Why did he pray for direction and help? Because he grasped the reality of his own need. As a shepherd boy, David learned to trust God when protecting his flock from dangerous animals. While still a teenager, he faced the giant soldier, Goliath, with only a sling. As a young man, he spent years running from King Saul, who had once been his friend. He lived in danger from the Philistines throughout adulthood. In later life, two of his own children (Absalom and Adonijah) sought to take his throne by violence. Though he lived in crisis, David became a man after God's own heart (1 Samuel 13:14), a man God deeply loved. Even when he sank to the very depths of sin (2 Samuel 11), he rebounded and received the forgiveness for which he longed. He prayed daily for practical direction, for he had tasted failure and he was well aware of his need.

Perhaps the best wisdom is learning from the mistakes of others and not making them yourself. Failing that, at least we can learn from our own poor choices and not repeat the same sin over and over again. *Someone said that we Christians all learn to pray eventually: the question is whether we will be praying for guidance, or forgiveness.* To re-state an old maxim, an ounce of guidance is worth more than a pound of forgiveness.

As a new Christian, I learned this lesson in the school of hard knocks. It seemed that every night my prayers would begin the same way: "Lord, forgive me for all my sins." Unfortunately, my list never included my failure to seek His guidance. The sin of presumptuousness is subtle but real, and it leaves millions of Christians living in mediocrity. *God wants us to go into the day with the benefit of His counsel, but all too often we end our day in needless defeat, simply because we have neglected to seek His direction.* God's guidance is as generously available as His forgiveness. He says, *"I will instruct you and teach you in the way which you should go; I will counsel you with My eye upon you."* (Psalm 32:8)

DRY SPELLS

No matter how much you love the Lord or the depth of your dedication, there will be times of spiritual dryness in your life. Usually these will merely be the result of physical fatigue. On other occasions, they may be the result of boredom, unresolved conflicts, medical difficulties, or unconfessed sin. David suffered acutely from middle-aged boredom, and Moses chafed under the unending ingratitude of those to whom he ministered. No one is exempt from times of spiritual dryness. Though these periods are not desirable, God can use them to teach you valuable lessons. It is often as a result of these occasions that you can most clearly see His faithfulness.

How can dry times be avoided? Consistency is the key! A good athlete does not work out only when he feels like it. He trains daily, because he knows that exercise is in his best interest and will make the difference in winning or losing to his competition. The same is true with farming or any other worthwhile activity. The Bible says, *"Let us not become weary in doing good, for at the proper time we will reap a harvest if we do not give up."* (Galatians 6:9, NIV)

Let's assume that you make a spiritual commitment to keep growing, but miss your Quiet Time for some good reason. The devil will try to turn that perfectly legitimate situation into the beginning of a dry spell. His tactics will probably operate something like this: he'll say, "If you really were a dedicated Christian, you would have gotten up this morning and had your Quiet Time. You made a commitment to spend time with God, and this morning you didn't do it." He will carefully avoid the fact that you stayed up late the night before doing something important which was spiritually on target. If you are in the will of God staying up late, you can also be in the will of God sleeping late! You need to memorize this verse: *"There is therefore now no condemnation for those who are in Christ Jesus."* (Romans 8:1) Satan does not have the right to condemn you as a Christian, because you do not belong to him. You are God's child.

Have you ever given your neighbor's child a spanking? It is a hazardous venture, because only your most discerning friends will appreciate and affirm your helping them with discipline. Many people would be offended by it. By and large, we spank our own children because they are our own responsibility. In the same way, the Bible says, *"God chastises those whom He loves."* (Hebrews 12:6a, Paraphrased) God gives us our spiritual spankings because we are His and He loves us. Satan has no right to administer correction, condemnation, or anything else to you as a Christian; so be careful not to let him discourage you as you walk with Christ.

A seminary professor once shared a principle which has been extremely helpful to me over the years. He taught me that "God convicts in specifics...and Satan condemns in generalities." For example, if you missed several Quiet Times for poor reasons, Satan might say, "Jim, you just don't have what it takes to be dedicated. To be honest, I don't think you are going to make it. If you really loved God, you'd do better." Satan will try to condemn you and make you feel defeated. Count on it. It's predictable!

In contrast, the Holy Spirit might say something like this, "Jim, you are My child and I love you, but you missed a real blessing this morning. I had something special to share with you from My Word. Be careful not to keep missing these times together, because you will not receive a blessing if you're not there."

God will always call attention to your omission, and He will also convict you about the need to correct the problem, but He will never condemn you for committing the sin. Satan will condemn you as a person because he wants to erode your self-worth. In contrast, God will convict you about the sinfulness of an act, but at the same time He will continually affirm you as a person and build your self-worth.

Failing to understand this basic difference has caused many people to get the activities of God and Satan mixed up. God operates out of concern with man's best interest at heart, but Satan plays by a different set of game rules. His desire is to weaken your witness and to entice you into an undisciplined lifestyle of spiritual compromise. He uses condemnation as a tool to achieve his purpose. He wants you to be negative about yourself, your friends, the church, the Bible, and if possible – even about life itself. His objective is to get you discouraged so you will quit trying to grow.

Be smart and remember that the enemy has no power over you whatsoever unless you give it to him of your own free will. *"There is therefore now no condemnation for those who are in Christ Jesus."* (Romans 8:1) We fight a defeated enemy, and *"We are more than conquerors through Him who loved us."* (Romans 8:37b, NIV) The secret of achieving godliness can be found in a lifestyle of spiritual consistency. The matchless life which has been made possible through Christ's death and suffering is already ours potentially, and it becomes ours experientially as we choose it on a day-to-day basis. What kind of life do you really want? This is the issue. Everything required for your happiness has already been provided. You are free as God's child to live a life of incomparable victory! The Scriptures declare, *"I press on toward the goal for the prize of the upward call of God in Christ Jesus."* (Philippians 3:14)

CHAPTER 5

PRINCIPLES FOR LIVING IN VICTORY

"But in all these things we overwhelmingly conquer through Him who loved us." (Romans 8:37)

PRINCIPLE #1: Growth Comes Slowly

"And let endurance have its perfect result, that you may be perfect and complete, lacking in nothing." (James 1:4)

As newlyweds, my wife and I had the unique experience of being houseguests of the Billy Grahams on Christmas Day. My spiritual dad, Grady Wilson, and Billy Graham, his lifelong friend, decided to play golf that afternoon. In order not to reveal my poor golf game, I quickly volunteered to be Dr. Graham's caddy. He had recently had surgery and seemed pleased with the suggestion. As we covered the mountainous North Carolina course, I took every opportunity to ask questions. Once when he sliced the ball, I said something like, "Life is sometimes like that, isn't it?" to which he replied, "Yes, some go off to the left, and others to the right." He described how those who move to either extreme diminish their own capacity for letting God use them in life.

We walked and talked, and I asked him if there were still many verses in the Bible that gave him trouble. He said there were some which he had been praying to understand for over twenty-five years. He went on to express an amazing truth – that when you really need to understand a passage, "God opens it up and it blossoms like a beautiful flower. In His own time, He reveals the hidden meaning and beauty of each facet of His Word."

Jesus illustrated this truth in His model prayer (Matthew 6:9-13). He taught us to pray in an attitude of patience. He didn't say, "Give us this day our full week's bread in advance." We were told to trust Him for one day at a time. Spiritually speaking, daily bread is God's only means of provision. When the Lord called Himself the *"bread of life"* (John 6:35), He sought to deepen our understanding of the reality that our daily bread is spiritual as well as physical. He said, *"Man does not live on bread alone, but on every word that comes from the mouth of God."* (Matthew 4:4b, NIV)

For most of us, eating is enjoyable. On the average, we eat about a thousand meals each year. The physical changes produced by eating take place so slowly that from one day to the next they cannot be seen. But our bodies are never static. Each day we change. Remember the impatience of childhood? Next year seemed an eternity away. Only as we mature do we come to understand that both spiritual and physical growth come slowly.

PRINCIPLE #2: Use Common Sense

Old-fashioned common sense is a virtue which will help insure a life of spiritual victory. For fun, imagine I am walking down a street in your town and you see tears streaming down my cheeks. Concerned, you ask, "Billie, why are you crying? You look so sad!" Forlornly I reply, "I missed lunch!" I say, "I made a commitment years ago to be an eater. I promised to be consistent! But today I blew it; I missed lunch. I just don't have what it takes. I'm through; I'll never eat again."

If you miss a meal, you simply compensate for it later. You do not stop eating. If you miss your daily Quiet Time, the same principle applies. Simply have a longer prayer time and more Bible reading later. This could be that night, or even the next morning.

There is nothing legalistic about eating your favorite meal. Why?

Because eating is a pleasure. Just as your physical hunger reminds you to visit the refrigerator, your spiritual hunger reminds you to read the Bible. *Self-imposed starvation and malnutrition are as foolish spiritually as they are physically, so use common sense and feed yourself.*

PRINCIPLE #3: Guard Your Affections

Some time ago, I was talking with a fellow minister about the importance of Christ being first place in our lives. Matthew 6:33 says, *"Seek ye first the kingdom of God . . ."* (KJV) I asked, "What do you think this verse really means?" I will never forget his answer. He said, "Billie, Christ doesn't mean first place in a traditional sense. What if you went home to your wife and said, 'I want you to know how much I love you. You are first place in my life. However, I want you to know about Mary Lou, Jane, Rose, and Jeanette. They are in second, third, fourth, and fifth place!'" I got the point. Do you think my wife would be happy just being in first place? Not at all. A wife or husband wants to be your only sweetheart, not just the first one on the list.

This is the spirit of Matthew 6:33. Christ wants to be first, and He wants to be all. His call to discipleship is always clear and always has been. He said, *"Unless you love Me more than your father, your mother, your wife, and your own life also, you cannot be My disciple."* (Luke 14:26, Paraphrased) This was not a new teaching but an echo of the first commandment, *"Love the Lord your God with all your heart and with all your soul and with all your mind."* (Matthew 22:37, NIV) As we learn to love God with all that we are, He can begin to love others through us. Because He lives in us, there is an inexhaustible supply of love available for us to share with those close to us, and those around the world. In his parting challenge in the Upper Room, He reminded His disciples of His new commandment: *"...love one another, even as I have loved you..."* (John 13:34)

Spiritual victory is achieved by allowing God to re-order our priorities and affections. In Colossians 3:2, Paul instructed us with these words, *"Set your mind on the things above, not on the things that are on earth."* If you want to find out if Christ is in first place, examine three areas of your life: your thoughts, your time, and your giving.

YOUR THOUGHTS

What do you enjoy thinking about? In Philippians 2:5, you are challenged to *"Let this mind be in you, which was also in Christ Jesus."* (KJV) The text goes on to say that the Lord humbled Himself to become a servant. Do you enjoy thinking of new ways to serve Him? In Philippians 4:8, the Bible says, *"Finally, brethren, whatever is true, whatever is honorable, whatever is right, whatever is pure, whatever is lovely, whatever is of good repute, if there is any excellence and if anything worthy of praise, let your mind dwell on these things."* Your mind is a mirror of your affections. When you truly seek His kingdom, you will know it. Your own thoughts will reveal it.

The Scriptures teach us this important principle: As a man *"thinks within himself, so he is."* (Proverbs 23:7a) We become like the things we think about. For this reason, the Bible says, *"Above all else, guard your heart, for it is the wellspring of life."* (Proverbs 4:23, NIV) You may be asking, "How do I guard my heart?" When the Bible refers to the heart, it is usually a reference to that part of your mind where life's deepest decisions are made. This is also the place where your affections are formed. *In a spiritual sense, you are guarding your heart when you guard your mind. It is a matter of both mental and spiritual hygiene.*

The Scripture warns, *"If anyone loves the world, the love of the Father is not in him."* (1 John 2:15b) This teaching is easy to understand in light of the First Commandment, *"Love the Lord your God with all your heart."* (Mark 12:30a) As a person gives his love to God, he has less left for the sinful things in the world around him.

YOUR TIME

Do you enjoy being with God in times of fellowship, recreation, worship, and training? The first Christians completely reordered their lives. They left everything they had to spend every possible hour with the Master. In those periods together, He taught them how to be *"fishers of men."* Mark 3:14a says, *"And He appointed twelve, that they might be with Him ..."* Their great service to the world followed the time spent in His presence.

Though the radical nature of the apostles' calling in most cases will not resemble the specific way God deals with you, the spirit of your calling is the same as Peter's, James', and John's. To them, their time with Christ was so valuable that they climbed mountains and walked the long, winding, dusty roads of Judea and Galilee to be near Him. (Matthew 17:1)

It is sobering to think that some Christians who look forward to heaven, will not rise fifteen minutes early or attend services on Sunday to be with Him here on earth. I have often wondered what it is people expect to experience in heaven that makes them think they want to go there. If they do not cherish the music of praise and the fellowship of His children, or love to hear the eternal truths of His Word, how strange the surroundings of heaven will seem.

The apostle John, describing that future time says, *"And I heard, as it were, the voice of a great multitude. . . as the sound of mighty peals of thunder, saying, 'Hallelujah! For the Lord our God, the Almighty, reigns.'"* (Revelation 19:6) Every moment spent praising Him and getting to know Him at the deepest human level is time that will have eternal value, because your relationship with Him will last forever. If you find yourself too busy for that kind of fellowship, you are too busy!

YOUR GIVING

"Where your treasure is, there will your heart be also." (Luke 12:34) *If you want to know what is important to you, look at your checkbook stubs.* Most of us are afraid to do that because we do not want to face the truth. They would show that our highest motivation and true goal for making money is not really the Great Commission. Our affections are still earthbound. We may suspect this and sometimes even grow a little concerned about it, but God cannot use us mightily, nor trust us as He would like to, until the "Goliath of ownership" has been slain in our lives.

As your daily Quiet Time becomes consistent and you begin to understand the principles on which God operates, you will discover that giving is at the very heart of His nature. Your personal spiritual growth can be measured by the answer to this question: "How much am I becoming like Him?" As you are conformed to His image, your new attitude will resemble that of David's day: *". . . the people rejoiced because they had offered so willingly, for they made their offering to the Lord with a whole heart."* (1 Chronicles 29:9)

Soon this will dawn on you: every moment of your life, every possession you value, every friendship you hold dear, every accomplishment you have achieved have come to you only through God's love. When this dawning occurs, you will be overwhelmed! You will be gripped with the desire to give back to Him in return. Did He not give you the mind, the will, and the strength to make everything you do and have possible?

The psalmist says, *"The earth is the Lord's, and all it contains, the world, and those who dwell in it."* (Psalm 24:1) Christ owns the 100 percent; yet He generously gives us 90 percent to invest, enjoy, and live on. The tithe, 10 percent of our income, is all that He requires, but a Christian's most joyful giving is often done well beyond that minimum. Why? Because of the knowledge that these funds will be used to help fulfill the Great Commission and bring the Good News of Jesus Christ to every nation of the world (Matthew 28:19; Matthew 24:14).

In Chapter 29 of First Chronicles, you will discover a fact which has always struck me as humorous, even though David expressed these thoughts in sincere worship and praise. In verse 12 he says, *"Both riches and honor come from Thee. . ."* and then, *"who am I and who are my people that we should be able to offer as generously as this? For all things come from Thee, and from Thy hand we have given Thee."* (verse 14)

The only thing we have to give God is what He has already given us. This is why we can never overgive or outgive God. One of my close friends says, "When we give to God, He is also giving to us. He just uses a bigger shovel!"

One Father's Day, I had an experience which brought this message home. My ten-year-old, Heather, decided to go shopping. For two years she had saved the money we had given her for making good grades. When I walked through the door, there were house slippers, pajamas, a robe, a new shirt, a tie (not a tie I would have picked, but a modern tie she thought I needed), and a shaving kit. The shaving kit contained soap, perfume, shaving lotion, and just about everything you could want. She was standing there beaming with delight! I picked her up, hugged her, and thanked her from the bottom of my heart. Then I asked, "Honey, how much did you spend?" (a typical father's question). The reply was, "Everything I had." I thought to myself, *"How impractically wonderful!"*

Love is like that. Do you think I would ever knowingly let

Heather go broke or suffer for having given me everything she had? Obviously, as her father, I have the power to give her back what she gave me many times over. What thrills me is the fact that she did the giving on her own, and that she did all she could. That, I will never forget.

So the deepest truth about giving is that both the 10 percent and the 90 percent are actually His. Everything you are is His. When your unrighteousness was exchanged for His goodness (2 Corinthians 5:21), the title deed of your life was passed to God forever (1 Corinthians 6:19). Your physical body became His earthly temple. You were no longer your own, for you had been bought with a price (1 Corinthians 6:20). From that point forward, you were treated as His very own child. When you try to shower Him with your love and your gifts, though they may seem large to you, they are never more than a small fraction of what He has already given. Why does God rejoice in our giving? Not because He needs it, but because He wants to see us become like Him. And He – is a giver! *"For God so loved the world that He gave. . ."* (John 3:16)

PRINCIPLE #4: CARVE ISLANDS IN YOUR DAY

"But the news about Him was spreading even farther, and great multitudes were gathering to hear Him and to be healed of their sicknesses. But He Himself would often slip away to the wilderness and pray." (Luke 5:15 & 16) The news about Christ was spreading. His ministry was growing and His responsibilities were increasing. When the pressures of life begin to build, we are presented with two options. We can either control our circumstances, or we can allow them to control us. The Lord Jesus modeled the right decision.

Paradoxically, the more you have to do, the less time you have to do it in. Recently I had lunch with a famous Bible teacher who is in much demand throughout the world. He said "Billie, I have a tremendous frustration in my life because this year I have received 2,000 invitations to speak. It is hard for me to know which of them the Holy Spirit intends for me to accept." As the impact of his ministry has increased, his need for wisdom and guidance has increased in direct proportion.

We have already discussed the importance of beginning your day with God. However, the Lord not only started His day in prayer, but as one busy businessman has put it, He "carved islands in His day." At every opportunity, He would slip away to be with the Father.

Even on the most noted day of His public ministry, Jesus planned ahead to have an island of time alone. Having fed 5,000 men and their families with only five loaves and two fish, He spoke to the multitudes *". . . teaching them many things."* (Mark 6:34, NIV) It was late in the day when the disciples picked up twelve baskets of broken pieces of bread and fish. Immediately, the Scripture says, *". . . He made His disciples get into the boat and go ahead of Him to the other side (of the Sea of Galilee) to Bethsaida, while He Himself was sending the multitude away. And after bidding them farewell, He departed to the mountain to pray."* (Mark 6:45 & 46)

Jesus broke all precedent on this occasion. Normally, He would have dismissed the multitude and taken the twelve to some quiet spot where they could talk together about His teachings. On this occasion however, He purposely separated Himself from the twelve. The only way for Him to be alone was to plan His day and make the circumstances compatible with His will. Because the twelve always pressed for His time and attention, He sent them away in order to have seasons alone with the Father. After dismissing the multitude, He carried through with His plan to have a Quiet Time. He went up on the mountain and spent the evening in prayer. He was in control of His life.

Mark wrote, *"And when it was evening, the boat was in the midst of the sea, and He was alone on the land. And seeing them straining at the oars, for the wind was against them, at about the fourth watch of the night, He came to them, walking on the sea; and He intended to pass by them."* (Mark 6:47 & 48) We are all familiar with the miracle of His walking on the water as He crossed the Sea of Galilee, but have you ever stopped to consider the reason He did it? Every activity of that late afternoon and night was calculated to serve His purpose. He did not walk on water as a public miracle to be gazcd at. IIe even intended to pass His own disciples by. The one and only reason this miracle was necessary, was the supreme importance He attached to being alone in prayer. You and I cannot walk on water to have a Quiet Time, but we can make provision for being alone with God as Jesus did.

How can we follow His example in today's world? For starters, we can cut the radio off in the car and use travel time for prayer and meditation. We can listen to cassettes of the Bible while walking or jogging, call a moratorium on excessive TV viewing, and create an atmosphere of quiet in our lives. Much of man's noise is a form of escapism by which he attempts to fill his loneliness. For the Christian, islands of quiet are times for listening, planning, fellowship, and peace of mind.

The great decisions of Jesus were normally made during these private times. His twelve apostles were chosen after a full night of prayer (Luke 6:12). And the greatest victory of His life was accomplished in solitary agony as He prayed, *"Not what I will, but what You will."* (Mark 14:32-36, NKJV) If it had not been for the triumph at Gethsemane, there would have been no Calvary.

Ultimately, the forgiveness of our sins was made possible as the result of Jesus' unfailing commitment to carve islands in His day for prayer. It was through this practice that He lived in unbroken obedience and perfect fellowship with the Father. That same provision is available for each one of us. James says, *"If any of you lacks wisdom, let him ask of God, who gives to all men generously. . ."* (James 1:5a) If we fail to take advantage of this provision, it is simply an evidence that we *"have not because we ask not."* (James 4:2b, KJV)

Who will suffer if we fail to carve islands in our day? If Jesus had failed, He would have forfeited His destiny, but we would have been the ones to suffer. The same concept holds true today. *If we fail to listen, we forfeit our ministry, but those we could have reached for Christ will pay the greatest price for our spiritual indifference.*

PRINCIPLE #5: Put Others First

The Scripture says, *"Do for others what you want them to do for you."* (Matthew 7:12, LB) With this Golden Rule in mind, let's pose a question: *what if you were depending upon someone like you to explain the plan of salvation to you? What would be the likelihood of your learning how to go to heaven?* Would you want their prayer life of intercession on your behalf to be like yours? Would you want their discipline and knowledge of the Bible to resemble yours? How about their love? Would you want their level of concern for your eternal destiny to be equated with the burden you have for others?

If your honest answers to these questions are "No," then you will understand why God wants to produce major changes in the quality of your life. People mattered to Jesus. For this reason, He strove to be everything they needed. He said, *"I have come not to be ministered unto but to minister."* (Mark 10:45, Paraphrased) He reminded us that a student is not above his teacher (Matthew 10:24a). He showed us how to bear witness at every turn in life by reaching down to the defeated like the woman at the well (John 4:4-26), and challenging intellectuals like Nicodemus (John 3:1-15). We are called to do the same.

If you were a greedy swindler like Zacchaeus (Luke 19), a leader like Lazarus (John 11), a man of wealth like Joseph of Arimathea (Matthew 27:57), a rebel like Paul (Acts 8), a common fisherman like Peter (Matthew 4:18), a timid teenager like John Mark (Acts 13:13), an immoral woman like Mary Magdalene (Luke 8:2), or a tender woman of faith like Mary of Bethany (John 11), – how would you want to be treated? Would you want someone to share the Gospel of Christ with you?

As we look at the several billion who populate our world, and consider the small percentage who have received Christ as their Lord and Savior, this question becomes extremely personal. Put yourself in their position—confused, lonely, or even bitter. At best, they have a very limited understanding of what God might be like. Living without Christ, their minds are focused on things that are material. Paul says, *". . . those who live as their human nature tells them to, have their minds controlled by what nature (flesh) wants. . ."* (Romans 8:5a, Good News) This results in spiritual death.

Jesus said, *"I came that they might have life, and might have it abundantly."* (John 10:10b) Because people were His purpose for coming to earth, as He lives through us, they will become our purpose as well. The apostle Paul explains how we learn to put people first when he declares, *"For it is God who is at work in you, both to will and to work for His good pleasure."* (Philippians 2:13)

If you want to live in victory, the ultimate means for this adventure is Christ Himself. No list of principles, however true they may be, will insure the quality of life which you desire. But be assured that victory is yours for the taking, because the One who lives in you is victorious. Rely upon Him to live out His resurrected life – *through* you. He is more than adequate for every trial and opportunity in your future. As you review these five principles, decide to let Him live them out through you on a daily basis.

QUIET TIME
READINGS

1 – 30

QUIET TIME 1

How can you *know* for certain that you are a Christian and that you have eternal life?

 Let's look at 1 John 5:11-13. *". . . God has given us eternal life, and this life is in His Son. He who has the Son has life; he who does not have the Son of God does not have life. I write these things to you who believe in the name of the Son of God so that you may know that you have eternal life."* (NIV)

Because God loves you, He wants you to enjoy a life filled with inner peace and confidence! He has given you His promise of eternal life from the very moment of your conversion until – forever. That's the good news proclaimed in the Bible.

Christ's death and resurrection have made it possible for you to be in a right relationship with God, both now and forever. The Bible calls this relationship eternal life. Because you received Jesus Christ as your Lord and Savior, you can *know* that you will be a part of God's family throughout eternity!

This assurance is not based upon your feelings, but upon God's promise. The Bible says, *"Yet to all who received Him, to those who believed in His name, He gave the right to become children of God."* (John 1:12, NIV)

Scriptural Insight	*Prayer*
I can be confident that I have eternal life because of God's promises in the Bible.	*Father, thank You for making me a Christian and giving me eternal life.*

QUIET TIME 2

How was your salvation made possible?

 The apostle Paul gave the answer to this question: *"For by grace you have been saved through faith, and that not of yourselves; it is the gift of God, not of works, lest anyone should boast."* (Ephesians 2:8 & 9, NKJV)

These verses clearly explain how you were saved, so read them again and circle the words *"by grace"* and *"not of works."* Think about the meaning of these important words. *"Grace"* literally means the kind of love that is undeserved and can never be earned.

Once a famous Christian was approached by one of the world's wealthiest men. The billionaire said, "I would give anything to have the *peace* you talked about today." The Christian replied, "I am sure that's true, but would you be willing to receive the peace of salvation if it cost you *nothing?*" The wealthy man was perplexed by the question. In daily life he was able to take credit for all his possessions and accomplishments because he had worked for them. The idea of receiving forgiveness as a "gift" from God seemed strange.

It is our pride that makes us want to get to heaven by our own efforts. Solomon, the wisest man in ancient history, was once inspired by God to write these words: *"Pride comes before a fall."* The Bible says salvation can *never* be achieved through works. Why? Because if we ever earned it, we would become proud and boastful!

Let's examine another truth. Since salvation cost the Lord everything, it costs you nothing. But, even if you had been willing to give *everything you had,* still you could not have purchased it! No amount of human effort or wealth would have been enough. Your salvation was a *perfect* gift from a *perfect* donor!

Scriptural Insight	Prayer
My salvation was given to me as a gift. I did not earn it.	*Father, thank You for Your grace that enabled me to become a Christian.*

QUIET TIME 3

What does the Bible teach about the Lord's ability to keep us once we are saved?

 Jesus once said, *"My sheep hear My voice, and I know them, and they follow Me; and I give eternal life to them, and they shall never perish; and no one shall snatch them out of My hand. My Father, who has given them to Me, is greater than all; and no one is able to snatch them out of the Father's hand."* (John 10:27-29)

Jesus is referring to Christians as sheep. The security of the sheep is not in *their* ability to defend themselves but in their *shepherd's* ability to protect them. God is the only one who is able to keep us secure. We are depending upon His ability, not our own. No one can take you out of your heavenly Father's hand, because He is more powerful than anyone anywhere, and it is He who has given you eternal life!

Assurance comes from knowing that when you become His child, you are His *forever*. To plant this wonderful truth in your mind, imagine that you are holding a coin in the palm of your left hand. Now close your hand, making a fist. Next, grip your left wrist with your right hand. Is there any way to drop the coin?

Reread paragraph one. Whose hands are you in? The Bible says you are securely held by both the *Father* and the *Son*.

Scriptural Insight	Prayer
I can be confident that I will always be a Christian.	*Father, thank You for your power and protection that holds me securely in the palm of Your hand.*

QUIET TIME 4

Have you noticed a change in your attitudes since you gave your life to Christ?

 2 Corinthians 5:17 says, *"Therefore, if anyone is in Christ, he is a new creation; the old has gone, the new has come!"* (NIV)

You are *not* the same person you were before you received Christ. Why? Because now, He is showing you the things in life that please Him; and even more important than that, He is causing you to *desire* these new virtues. This is the kind of supernatural change that comes from deep within.

Once a communist who spoke in a city park promised a new *coat* to every listener who would embrace his political doctrine. At the close of the speech, a Christian asked for equal time. He countered the offer by promising that God would put a new *man* in every coat if they would repent of their sins and place their faith in Jesus Christ!

The world is primarily interested in new and better coats, but God is interested in new and better men!

In the New Testament, when the hated tax collector, Zacchaeus, became Christ's disciple, he returned to the same house in the same clothes on the same day, but he was a new man. The inner change had taken place. A new life had begun!

The Christian message is always *good news*. When a person decides he really wants to change, what a joy it is to learn that God has already provided a way!

Scriptural Insight	Prayer
You have made me into a new creation because I have received You into my life.	*Father, thank You for the change you have made in me since becoming a Christian.*

QUIET TIME 5

How does work fit into the process of spiritual growth? If salvation is a gift from God, what is my responsibility?

 The apostle Paul once wrote, *"And let us not lose heart in doing good, for in due time we shall reap if we do not grow weary."* (Galatians 6:9)

Being tired because of energy expended in doing good is to be expected. The Lord Himself was weary on many occasions, but being tired of *doing good* is *not* an acceptable option for a Christian. We are called to follow His example of consistent service. He said, *"...he who believes in Me, the works that I do he will do also..."* (John 14:12b, NKJV)

Once a high-society crowd in formal dress eagerly awaited a performance by the famous composer and pianist, Ignace Jan Paderewski. A small boy, restless with waiting, slipped away from his parents, went to the stage and began playing "Chopsticks" on the grand piano. Hearing the angry roar that rose from the audience, Paderewski hurried to the stage unannounced. He leaned over the boy and began to play a beautiful counter melody which harmonized with the simple tune. As he played, he whispered in the boy's ear, "You're doing good. Keep on playing – don't quit."

Your first efforts in serving the Lord may seem simple and faltering, but you can rest assured that your willingness will be crowned with success if you faithfully continue.

This is the summarized message we have from God: Don't stop! If misunderstood, do good; if unappreciated, do good; if tired from years of service, keep doing good! Don't cease doing My work in the world!

Scriptural Insight	Prayer
Now that I am a Christian, I want to find some way to serve God out of love.	*Father, please show me some way that I can be of help at our church.*

QUIET TIME 6

Why attend church?

Hebrews 10:24 & 25a says, *". . . and let us consider how to stimulate one another to love and good deeds, not forsaking our own assembling together, as is the habit of some, but encouraging one another..."*

When Christians come together for worship, we *share* our strength, faith, and understanding. It is in this fellowship that we seek to grow in the likeness of Christ. Church is not a *place* – it is a group of forgiven people who are attempting to carry out God's plan for their lives.

Encouragement – What a powerful word. It is the essence of brotherly love. Christians are called to meet together for the purpose of stimulating one another to *"love and good deeds."* We need to be supportive when problems come and affirm the importance of each other's strengths and abilities.

The giant redwood trees on the West Coast of the United States are among the oldest and largest trees in the world. Many of them have stood for centuries against the onslaughts of nature, but what is the secret of their great strength? It is not the depth of their roots – in fact, they have a very shallow root system for their size. The answer is hidden in the fact that these mammoth trees stand close enough together for their roots to intertwine. This *bond* of unity gives them the ability to stand against the most violent storms.

The amazing endurance of the church, in spite of tremendous persecution, testifies to the importance of studying God's Word, praying, singing, laughing, and even crying together!

Scriptural Insight	*Prayer*
It is very important for me to attend church.	*Father, thank You for the people at my church and for the help they have been to me.*

QUIET TIME 7

What does the Bible teach us about time management?

 "And the whole city had gathered at the door. And He healed many who were ill. . . [and the next day,] in the early morning, while it was still dark, He arose and went out and departed to a lonely place, and was praying there." (Mark 1:33, 34a, 35)

It was after a very busy day of serving that Jesus got up early to spend time alone with His heavenly Father. When you face hectic days, reflect on His example. Notice that He lived according to a set of *priorities* that were out of step with the rest of the world. *Every activity,* even activities *for* God, had to take second place to His time alone *with* God.

What would happen if you decided to live like that? You would enjoy the uncommon qualities of peace, certainty, and wisdom that characterize those who prioritize their time the way He did.

In the New Testament, a lady named Martha once worked hard serving as the Lord's hostess, while her sister Mary sat at His feet and listened to His teachings. Why did Jesus compliment Mary, saying she had *"chosen the good part?"* (Luke 10:42b) Because she valued *time* with Him in the same way that He valued *time* with His Father.

To be truly effective in Christian service, you must learn how to *distinguish* between the *good* and the *best.* Even worthwhile activities will begin taking second place to your time alone with God. The further you go, the more you will desire to devote yourself to Bible reading and prayer.

Scriptural Insight	*Prayer*
I need to always make it a priority to spend time with God every morning.	*Father, help me to be disciplined and consistent to spend time with You each morning so I can keep growing spiritually.*

QUIET TIME 8

What happens if I sin now that I am saved?

First, it is important to remember that the Lord's death on the cross was more than adequate to pay for any sin you have committed, or ever will commit. Second, God's Word says that He loves us and wants us to enjoy an *abundant life* on a daily basis. This is why He wants us to bring sins to Him the moment they occur. 1 John 1:9 says, *"If we confess our sins, He is faithful and just to forgive us our sins and to cleanse us from all unrighteousness."* (NKJV)

What does it mean to *confess* your sins? It means to *agree* with God in prayer about any attitude, motive, or action that displeases Him. When you sincerely seek to *renounce* your sin, He stands ready to forgive and cleanse you. Through this continual cleansing, your fellowship with God will stay fresh, and you will experience the full *joy of your salvation.*

God will not only *forgive* our sin when we honestly confess it, but will also *cleanse* and *purify* our hearts. This is His promise!

The following are five types of prayers that you may wish to consider when writing your prayer each morning:

Petition: "Lord, help me to. . ."
Thanksgiving: "Lord, thank you for. . ."
Adoration: "Lord, you are. . ."
Confession: "Lord, please forgive me for. . ."
Intercession: "Lord, please help. . ."

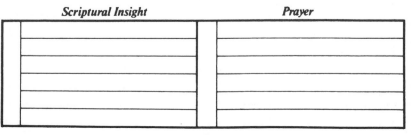

Scriptural Insight   *Prayer*

QUIET TIME 9

What if God wants me to do something, but I feel I'm unable?

The apostle Paul said, *"I can do all things through Christ who strengthens me. "* (Philippians 4:13, NKJV)

The adequacy of Christ is assured to every one of His disciples. He said, *"In the world you will have tribulation; but be of good cheer, I have overcome the world. "* (John 16:33b, NKJV) When God leads you to attempt something which seems impossible; this is merely His way of helping you mature in your faith.

The Lord will *never* call you to carry out a task unless *He* is already committed to doing it *through you.* In Christ, you are never limited to your own resources.

After a devastating tornado ripped through a Texas town, an extraordinary photograph appeared on the front page of the newspaper. It showed a piece of straw deeply imbedded in a telephone pole! Under normal circumstances, this could never have happened, but when impelled by the mighty power of a tornado, the fragile straw accomplished the impossible!

You will sometimes stand in amazement as the Lord begins to strengthen you. Once you were too timid, too weak, or too defeated to serve Him, but now you are a chosen vessel – called to a life of victory!

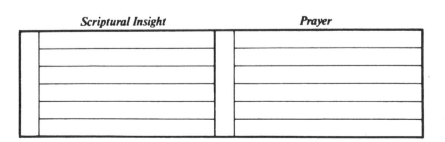

Scriptural Insight	*Prayer*

QUIET TIME 10

How can I start serving God in small ways?

Words are *important!* Proverbs 15:1 says, *"A gentle answer turns away wrath, but a harsh word stirs up anger."* (NIV) What we say can either accomplish great *good* or do great *harm.*

When was the last time you hurt someone by something you said? Do you remember the emotion and pain which you felt later as you considered your unkind words? The Bible says, *"For every species of beasts and birds, of reptiles and creatures of the sea, is tamed, and has been tamed by the human race. But no one can tame the tongue..."* (James 3:7 & 8a)

Consider the testimony of Isaiah 50:4: *"The Lord God has given Me the tongue of disciples, that I may know how to sustain the weary one with a word."*

What a privilege it is to speak when a word is needed! No one can fully estimate the positive impact a single comment can make when spoken at just the right time.

As a boy, one of North America's best-known authors was plagued by low self-esteem. One day in class, his essay was returned with these words written across the top of the page – Henry Wadsworth Longfellow! Those three words of encouragement symbolized a challenge which became the driving force behind his life.

Scriptural Insight	*Prayer*

QUIET TIME 11

Do you remember facing a temptation you felt you could not resist? Have you ever wondered if other people were tempted in the same way?

Paul answers that question: *"No temptation has overtaken you but such as is common to man; and God is faithful, who will not allow you to be tempted beyond what you are able, but with the temptation will provide the way of escape also, that you may be able to endure it."* (1 Corinthians 10:13)

The Bible says quite clearly that you *will face temptation.* Being a Christian doesn't alter that, but it does change the way you will react when tempted. Keep in mind that there is a great difference between temptation and sin. To be *tempted* is *not* a sin. Temptation is being lured to do something that is not God's will. Sin is the willful decision to yield to that temptation.

This verse contains three facts to remember when you are tempted. *First*, you are *not alone* in your battle. *Second,* God will *not allow* you to be tempted beyond your ability to resist. *Third,* God *always* provides a *"way of escape"* when you are under attack. No temptation is irresistible. The question is, "Are you *willing* to take the way out?"

Philippians 4:13 says, *"I can do all things through Christ . . . "* This includes choosing the right path when it is difficult. Each time a temptation presents itself, the first thing to look for is the "exit." When you are *willing*, all the power you need will be there to back up your right decision!

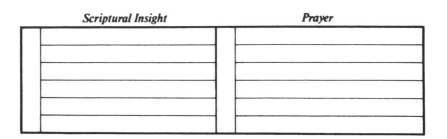

Scriptural Insight	Prayer

QUIET TIME 12

What well-known pitfalls should I look out for on my spiritual journey?

 In a self-centered world, you will constantly be tempted to draw attention to yourself. When the apostle Paul preached in the city of Corinth, he faced a similar temptation, so he consciously planned to uplift Christ and not himself. This is why he wrote, *". . . I determined to know nothing among you except Jesus Christ, and Him crucified."* (1 Corinthians 2:2)

This concept was beautifully illustrated when a veteran missionary once visited friends in Thailand. A magnificent orchid was displayed in the center of the host's dining table. The stunning blossom was often mentioned during the meal. Shortly after leaving the house, the missionary asked the other guests if they could remember the vase used for the centerpiece. No one could! The vase had been totally eclipsed by the *beauty* of the lovely flower.

When you are at your best spiritually, people's *attention* will be drawn to the Lord, not to you. It is the warmth of *His* presence that will linger in their minds.

What impression do you make when you receive recognition or compliments? Does the praise stop with you, or do you sincerely pass it on to Jesus? Remember that your life's mission is to draw the world's attention to Him.

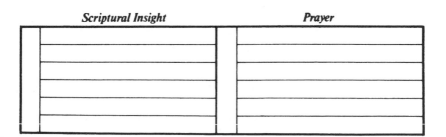

Scriptural Insight	*Prayer*

QUIET TIME 13

"You are the light of the world. . . Let your light shine before men in such a way that they may see your good works, and glorify your Father who is in heaven. " (Matthew 5:14a & 16) In the Bible, Christians are called *lights* or *lamps*. Around the world, light has the same purpose – it dispels the darkness!

Once a lady came to her pastor complaining about the factory where she was employed. She wanted to quit working there because nearly all the employees were non-Christians and they constantly used profanity. The pastor listened, then asked her, "Where do you put lights?" Disregarding the question, she complained about their wild parties, drinking, and dirty jokes. Again he asked, "But where do you put lights?"

Puzzled by his response, the lady went on to tell him that some of her associates at work were also involved in immoral relationships. A third time he questioned, "But where do you put lights?" Annoyed she said, "I don't know *where* you put lights. In dark places, I guess!" Suddenly, she realized what he had been trying to say.

The lady's attitude changed when she realized she was called to be the *light of Christ* in that dark situation.

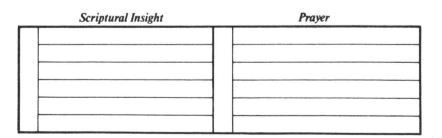

	Scriptural Insight		*Prayer*

QUIET TIME 14

". . . you have done well that you shared in my distress . . . For even in Thessalonica you sent aid once and again for my necessities." (Philippians 4:14 & 16, NKJV)

There are *two* important lessons to be learned in these verses. First, as Christians we are to give help to those in distress; and second, as Paul demonstrates, we are to express *gratitude* when we are helped.

One cold winter evening, two seminary students, Nat Spencer and his brother, walked along the banks of Lake Michigan. Suddenly, in the distance, they saw a large steamer begin to sink. Soon The Lady Elgin's 323 passengers were in the freezing waters!

Both Spencer brothers were strong athletes, but Nat was an especially good swimmer. Taking a rope in his hand, the brave student swam to the sinking ship. Fighting the frigid water again and again, he saved the lives of 23 people in this heroic feat; but because of his sacrifice, he spent the rest of his life as an invalid. Would you have expected those whom he rescued to *devote* themselves to meeting his needs? Tragically, he never heard from even *one* of them! Nat did his part, but 23 people *failed* to express their gratitude.

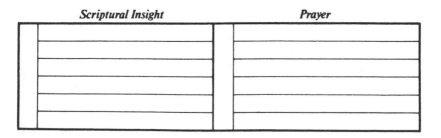

Scriptural Insight   *Prayer*

QUIET TIME 15

"As you therefore have received Christ Jesus the Lord, so walk in Him." (Colossians 2:6)

Initially you received Christ *by faith; continue* in that joy!

Years ago, a little boy begged his father to let him go to the circus which had come to town. After doing his chores, he was given a dollar bill and sent on his way. As he neared the fairgrounds, the circus parade was in progress. When the clown at the end of the parade passed by, the little boy placed his dollar in the clown's hand and went home happily, thinking he had seen the circus. Many Christians live just like this little boy; they mistake the beginning for the end!

The new birth is simply the gateway to a new life. As you learn to *walk by faith,* the world will be filled with wonderful new discoveries. Never become satisfied merely looking back to your conversion. Learn to walk with Him and run with Him. Be assured the best is *always* yet to come.

Paul expressed it this way: *". . . forgetting what lies behind and reaching forward to what lies ahead, I press on toward the goal for the prize of the upward call of God in Christ Jesus."* (Philippians 3:13b & 14) He lived for the future, not the past.

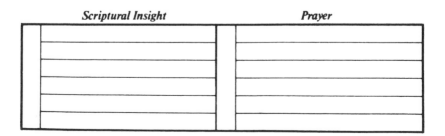

Scriptural Insight   *Prayer*

QUIET TIME 16
Read Psalm 27:11, 31:3, 32:8

The Bible and the indwelling Holy Spirit have been given to every redeemed child of God. Why? So we can *know* and *carry out* His will. Listen to His promise: *"I will instruct you and teach you in the way which you should go; I will counsel you with My eye upon you."* (Psalm 32:8)

God has not put us out to sea without a compass, nor on a journey without a map. To the contrary; we know *who* we are, *why* we are here, and *where* we are going.

The Bible teaches us about the ministry of the Holy Spirit, and it is the Holy Spirit who enables us to understand the Bible. So we need the *combined* help of both to clearly discern God's leading.

We gain knowledge, wisdom, and understanding through reading the Scriptures; but the assurance and inner peace that normally accompany our obedience are the work of the Holy Spirit.

Do you see the *balance?* If you are lopsided and do little Bible reading but spend much time in prayer, or vice versa, it will be more difficult for you to discern God's will.

Scriptural Insight	*Prayer*

Application: J. *will* . . .

QUIET TIME 17
Read Matthew 28:18-20

This was Jesus' final instruction to His disciples before returning to heaven. On the basis of His authority, both they and we were commanded to *"make disciples"* throughout the world.

The apostle Paul's clear awareness of being authorized for service stands out as a vivid example to every Christian. Consider his deep feeling of involvement in this passage: *". . . we are ambassadors for Christ . . . we implore you on Christ's behalf, be reconciled to God."* (2 Corinthians 5:20, NKJV)

You may never be asked to speak on behalf of a president or have the power of a government behind you, but as a Christian, you have a far greater privilege. In your home, your neighborhood, and every other place you influence, you are Christ's representative. Your mission is to call people back to God and make disciples for Jesus Christ.

When a young soldier named Alexander was found to be derelict in his duties, he was brought before Alexander the Great. The powerful king looked at the soldier and said, "Either change your ways or change your name!" When you represent Christ and bear His name, your authority is equaled by your responsibility.

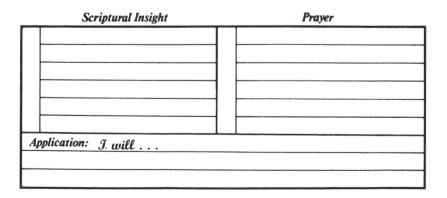

Scriptural Insight   *Prayer*

Application: I will . . .

QUIET TIME 18
Read Deuteronomy 6:5-7

We have been called to love God with all our hearts and to faithfully teach our children to do the same. How fortunate we are that this divine mandate is at the same time an invitation to *joy*. It is by keeping this First Commandment that we experience spontaneous happiness!

This is why John could say, *". . . His commandments are not burdensome."* (1 John 5:3b) It is never a burden to be asked to do something you truly enjoy. Imagine being asked to smell your favorite flower, eat your favorite dessert, or listen to your favorite music. Would you resist the invitation?

Loving God is sweeter, by far, than any human relationship. Why? Because He *never* misunderstands you, mistreats you, forgets you, or leaves you. He is always kind, merciful, and overflowing with life! He will never embarrass you with impurity or disappoint you by changing His character. He has promised to be consistently holy – to remain the same, *"yesterday, today, and forever."* (Hebrews 13:8, NKJV)

It is said that respect is the best foundation on which to build a lasting love. With this in mind, consider how *long* and how *deeply* you can love God.

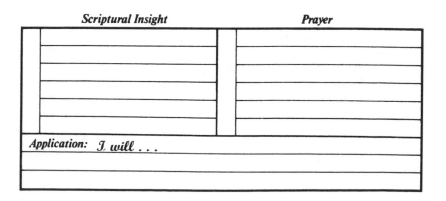

Scriptural Insight   *Prayer*

Application: *I will . . .*

QUIET TIME 19

Read 1 Corinthians 6:19 & 20 three times.

Quietly meditate on the remarkable truth that Christ lives *in* you! *"I have been crucified with Christ; and it is no longer I who live, but Christ lives in me; and the life which I now live in the flesh I live by faith in the Son of God, who loved me, and delivered Himself up for me."* (Galatians 2:20)

Properly understood, the Christian life is not living *for* Christ, but letting Christ live His abundant life *through* you. You are dead. That is to say, the sins which once held you captive have been *"crucified with Christ."* The old, strictly human "you" no longer lives. The life of faith which is now yours comes from His presence *within.* On the outside, you may look the same; but on the inside, new life has been present since the moment you invited Christ to reside in your heart.

The Christian life is not seeking to keep a set of rules to please God, nor is it a philosophy. It is the work of God's Spirit in our lives. This is why unsaved people find the Bible so hard to understand. The Bible says, *"But a natural man does not accept the things of the Spirit of God; for they are foolishness to him . . ."* (1 Corinthians 2:14a)

Living the Christian life without the indwelling power of Christ is impossible. This is why the Bible declares, *"Christ in you, the hope of glory."* (Colossians 1:27) It is the fact that He is *in* you that makes your Christian life a reality.

Scriptural Insight	*Prayer*

Application: *I will . . .*

QUIET TIME 20
Read Colossians 1:9-12

Have you ever attempted to pray for someone and not known what they really needed?

Paul's primary prayer request for his fellow Christians was that they might be filled with the knowledge of *God's will*. Why? Because this is what every person needs. Living in God's will is the secret to happiness in this life and the key to a *"Well done, thou good and faithful servant"* in the next!

Intercession focuses on seeking to help align a person with the will of God in a specific area of his life. Beyond this, it brings needs of every kind before the Lord. No subject is too small or too large for intercession; if the problem is of concern to you, it is of concern to your heavenly Father.

The apostle prayed for his fellow believers to receive wisdom and understanding. For the lost he prayed: *"My heart's desire and prayer to God for Israel is that they might be saved."* If you have Christian friends, pray for their spiritual and physical needs. If you have lost friends, ask the Lord to graciously convict them of their sins.

For more than fifty years, George Mueller, who was well-known for his ministry of intercession, prayed for five lost friends. After five years, the first one received Christ. In ten years, two more came to the Savior. Mueller persevered for twenty-five years, and the fourth man was saved. When the fifth man received Christ, the man of prayer was already in the presence of the King! Fifty-two years of intercession had produced its eternal fruit.

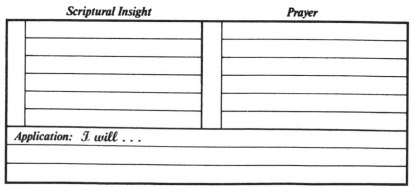

Scriptural Insight	*Prayer*

Application: I will . . .

QUIET TIME 21
Read 1 Thessalonians 5:12-18

"Rejoice always; pray without ceasing; in everything give thanks; for this is God's will for you in Christ Jesus." (1 Thessalonians 5:16-18)

How is this possible? As Christians, we can *"rejoice always"* because our joy does not spring from *outward* circumstances, but from the *indwelling* presence of Christ. It is our unique privilege to experience the warmth of divine love and *"peace that passes understanding."* Our *joy* is simply the by-product of this special quality of fellowship with the Father.

The term *"pray without ceasing"* does not mean to actually verbalize your prayers without stopping, but rather to maintain a spirit of prayer that pervades every part of your day. While driving your car, working in the kitchen, mowing the lawn, or exercising, you can enjoy inner dialogue with God and be fully conscious of His presence.

Perhaps you will better understand this concept when you stop to consider the portion of a good conversation that is spent in listening. Prayer is a wonderful two-way conversation in which you can talk to God, and He can talk to you; no one else will ever know what is being said unless you want them to. As the months go by, you will also discover that the better you know Him, the more natural it will be to pray continually.

"Giving thanks in everything" does not mean that we are to thank God *for* every thing that happens to us, but to live in an attitude of faith so we can give thanks *in* every circumstance we experience.

Scriptural Insight	*Prayer*

Application: *I will . . .*

QUIET TIME 22
Read 1 Peter 3:13-15

You have probably already experienced criticism and suffering for one reason or another, but has it been for *"righteousness' sake?"* The Bible says, *". . . to the degree that you share the sufferings of Christ, keep on rejoicing; . . .If you are reviled for the name of Christ, you are blessed, because the Spirit of glory and of God rests upon you."* (1 Peter 4:13a & 14)

When the early Christians were flogged for speaking about the Lord, they went out *"...rejoicing that they had been considered worthy to suffer shame for His name."* (Acts 5:41b)

You will probably be called a "do-gooder," a "holy Joe," and lots of other things when you take a stand for Christ. Jesus predicted this when He said, *"A servant is not above his master."* In His own lifetime, He was called a blasphemer, a glutton, and a demoniac. Why? Because He brought light into darkness, and *". . . everyone who does evil hates the light, and does not come to the light, lest his deeds should be exposed."* (John 3:20)

The Lord said, *"You are the light of the world."* Light is only popular with people who are happy about what they are doing. Stop to consider how much crime, drinking, and immorality occurs under the veil of darkness. It is plain to see why He used this illustration.

Peter has a word for us in 1 Peter 3:17: *"For it is better, if God should will it so, that you suffer for doing what is right rather than for doing what is wrong."* Being persecuted for what you do in the light is a form of suffering which is perfectly *acceptable* for a Christian!

Scriptural Insight	*Prayer*

Application: J. will . . .

QUIET TIME 23

Read Proverbs 15:16 & 17 three times.

"Better is a little" is a phrase that runs against the current of today's thinking about success!

We forget that Jesus said, *". . . a man's life does not consist in the abundance of his possessions."* (Luke 12:15b, NIV) In the early church, few Christians came from the ranks of nobility, wealth, or status. It was the common people who heard Jesus gladly.

If happiness were the result of having *much,* then drugs, alcoholism, ulcers, and divorce would be less prevalent among the wealthy in our society. To the contrary, great treasure without reverence for God only produces turmoil and dissipation.

The Bible warns that *". . . the love of money is a root of all kinds of evil."* (1 Timothy 6:10a) If a root of a man's sin is materialism, then increasing his income will only *add* to his problem. The key to enjoying prosperity is not to be found in prosperity itself! Rather, it comes from the fulfillment of *seeing* God accomplish His will through the means which He has placed in your hands.

Make this your goal: love God, not money, and do not covet the lifestyle of those around you who love money. Jesus said, *". . . seek first His kingdom and His righteousness; and all these things shall be added to you."* (Matthew 6:33, KJV)

Good news! When you have enthroned Christ as Lord and have acknowledged His ownership of your life, your joy will be *equally great,* whether you have little or much of this world's goods!

Scriptural Insight	*Prayer*

Application: I will . . .

QUIET TIME 24
Read Matthew 13:44-46

Jesus said the kingdom of heaven is like a costly treasure; something of supreme quality, worth everything one owns. On another occasion, He referred to His *teachings* as pearls and warned His disciples not to give things of value to those who were spiritually unprepared to receive them. It was for this reason that the Lord so frequently said, *"If anyone has ears to hear, let him hear."* By that He meant, "If you can appreciate the value of spiritual truth, then listen to what I am about to say." Today that same challenge is ours every time we read the Bible or hear a sermon.

A famous fable tells of three men traveling in a desert by night. Under the starlight they met a stranger. He told them they would be both glad and sorry if they took his advice and filled their pockets and saddlebags with the stones from a nearby river. The men were somewhat curious, but also quite skeptical; so when they reached the river, they took only a few of the stones. The next morning, they were "both glad and sorry," just as the man had said. The stones had turned into exquisite *pearls!* They were glad about the ones they had taken, but *sorry* about the ones they had left behind.

The cost of gaining spiritual insight has nothing to do with money. *Time* is the "price tag" for this investment of lasting value.

Timothy: You will notice that there are no more Scriptural insight, prayer, or application blanks at the bottom of your page. You may now start using the blanks provided in your *Spiritual Journal* in the Quiet Time Section on page 20.

QUIET TIME 25
Read 2 Timothy 3:16 & 17

God actually inspired the writing of the Bible. The term "inspired," or "God-breathed," means that it came from the mouth of God – and was what He wanted written. These verses present four valuable ministries of the Bible:

1. *Teaching* - It shows you God's plan for your life.
2. *Reproof* - It calls you to account when you sin.
3. *Correction* - It shows you how to correct your mistakes.
4. *Training in righteousness* - It shows you how to avoid sin in the future.

When you read the Bible on Monday, you may need *correction* because of a poor decision. However, on Tuesday you might be ready for God to *teach* you something totally fresh.

If you lived a hundred years and read the Bible every day, it would always be current. Billy Graham once said he had prayed about certain passages for 25 years and still did not fully understand their meaning; however, when the Lord knew he needed an explanation, the meaning of that passage would blossom like a beautiful flower whose season had finally come.

The Bible claims to be God's Word, and it has lived up to that claim across the centuries. Give it the sacred and holy place of honor that it rightfully deserves. Jesus said, *"Heaven and earth will pass away, but My words will never pass away."* (Matthew 24:35, NIV)

QUIET TIME 26

Read 2 Corinthians 9:6-13

Money is only a touchy subject to those who think they own it! The Bible reminds us that *"The earth is the Lord's, and all it contains, the world, and those who dwell in it."* (Psalm 24:1)

This simply means the clothes on your back, the car you drive, your house, the money in your bank account, and the very ground you walk upon are all His! Once this is understood, the ministry of giving is automatically seen in a whole new light.

God is merely allowing you and me the privilege of becoming involved in something which He deeply enjoys!

God is a giver, and as your Father, He wants you to become like Him. He gives bountifully, and He wants to teach you how to enjoy that same freedom.

He wants to "multiply your seed for sowing" and enrich your life through generous giving. The Bible says, *". . . God is able to make all grace abound to you, that . . . you may have an abundance for every good deed."* (2 Corinthians 9:8)

Do you still give *grudgingly*? Why? It shouldn't be hard to give away something that was *never* yours in the first place! Ask the Lord to remind you that you *own* nothing, and then begin trusting Him for real *joy* in giving.

Pause to look at your checkbook stubs; they will tell you volumes. The Bible says, *". . . where your treasure is, there will your heart be also."* (Matthew 6:21) Giving is the practical measure of our desire to become like our heavenly Father.

QUIET TIME 27
Read 1 Peter 5:8 & 9

Although Satan is a *defeated enemy* awaiting his final destruction, he still has *temporary power* to influence the lives of Christians and lost people here on earth. Peter describes him as *"a roaring lion,"* aggressively seeking his prey. In today's context, with blatant pornography, a soaring crime rate, profanity in the media, and the ever-present threat of war, his presence and activity are more evident than ever.

God's Word in this circumstance is – *"Resist the devil and he will flee from you."* (James 4:7b) You may be thinking, "How can this be done?" We are no match for Satan in our own strength, but with God's power working in and through us, we can indeed *". . .stand firm against the schemes of the devil."* (Ephesians 6:11b) Romans 8:31b boldly declares, *"If God be for us, who can be against us?"* (KJV) Like most bullies, Satan will cower in the face of a serious fight. Historically, it is Christians who have taken a stand on social and moral issues. We have been called to be salt and light in society!

On a personal level, you can decide *in advance* to say "no" to Satan's temptations as you daily reaffirm this decision. Resisting temptation will become a lifestyle. Each victory will become the foundation for added spiritual growth.

QUIET TIME 28

Read Philippians 1:6 three times.

When you received Christ as your Lord – you stepped into God's will. Now He wants to do something of lasting value in and through your life. His divine objective is to keep you *in a process* of positive change until you reach your full potential. Based on this truth, someone has said, "God loves us just the way we are, but He loves us *too* much to leave us that way!"

Paul expresses the same assurance, *". . . being confident of this, that He who began a good work in you will carry it on to completion . . ."* (Philippians 1:6a, NIV)

"For we are His workmanship, created in Christ Jesus for good works, which God prepared beforehand, that we should walk in them. " (Ephesians 2:10) This means all of us were made for ministry! Each and every person has the capacity to say "yes" or "no" to that destiny.

You have already made life's biggest and most important decision, but living in daily obedience to God's plan requires a second kind of commitment – the eagerness to *keep on growing.* Said another way, your fulfillment will be as complete as your willingness to let Him complete His "good work" in your life.

Have you ever marvelled at the beauty of a butterfly? He begins life as a slow, earthbound caterpillar, then is transformed by a process called *metamorphosis.* In the same way, when you said "Yes" to Christ, God began the process of *spiritual metamorphosis* in you. Meditate on this fact: slowly but surely, you are being changed to resemble the inner beauty of His Son, Jesus Christ!

QUIET TIME 29

Read Philippians 4:15-20

The Christians to whom Paul wrote had recently sent him gifts to assist in his ministry. Paul commended them for their generosity, which was *"pleasing to God."* He also reminded them that God would meet all their needs.

You can take comfort in knowing that God will supply your personal *"daily bread"* just as He provided for the Christians in Philippi. That does not mean you can be lazy or wait for a gift to be dropped out of the sky. It does mean that if you are responsible and obedient to God, you can depend on Him to take care of you.

Faith is trusting. Trust in His sufficiency, even when you cannot see how all your needs will be provided!

A parent understands that a child needs food, clothing, and shelter, so all of these things are provided. A small child does not think about where his next meal will come from or what clothing he will wear. Though he may never realize it, he is totally dependent upon his parents.

The picture becomes clear when you stop to look at it this way: just as an earthly parent takes pleasure in meeting his child's needs, so our heavenly Father takes pleasure in meeting ours.

QUIET TIME 30
Read 1 Thessalonians 5:19-28

Paul says, *"Now may the God of peace Himself sanctify you entirely; and may your spirit and soul and body be preserved complete, without blame at the coming of our Lord Jesus Christ. Faithful is He who calls you, and He also will bring it to pass."* (1 Thessalonians 5:23-24)

The same God who called you to salvation is in the process of making you holy. The Bible calls this *"sanctification"* or *"being conformed to the image of Christ."* Salvation has three tenses:

Past Tense	Present Tense	Future Tense
Your spirit was saved when you accepted Christ and were born again spiritually.	Your soul (or mind) *is being* saved daily as you are changed by the indwelling Christ.	Your body *will be* saved when it is transformed at Christ's glorious return.

Salvation began with an event called conversion, but each day your thought life, your home life, your school life, your vocational life, and your religious life are all being saved from what they would have been without His presence in your heart.

As if *this* were not enough, God has even more in store: In His kingdom, your body will at last be perfect and beyond the reach of pain, aging, or sin. How can this be true? Because the God who made you willed it to be so and committed Himself to *"bring it to pass."*

Timothy: Now that you have finished these Quiet Time readings, you will start receiving your Scriptural insights from the Bible only. First read pages 6 & 7 of your *Spiritual Journal*. These pages will show you *how* to continue having an effective daily Quiet Time from the Scriptures. Next, turn to page 109 in your *Timothy's Guide*. This Guide shows you *where to read* to continue enjoying your daily Quiet Times.

QUIET TIME READING GUIDE

"Thy word is a lamp to my feet, and a light to my path."
(Psalm 119:105)

Review pages 6 & 7 in your *Spiritual Journal* before you begin. Read the Scriptures with personal application in mind. As you read each morning, come before the Lord with these prayerful attitudes:

Petition: Lord, help me to . . .

Adoration: Lord, You are . . .

Thanksgiving: Lord, thank You for . . .

Confession: Lord, please forgive me for . . .

Use the notetaking section of your *Spiritual Journal* to record any questions about passages which you find difficult to understand during your daily Quiet Times. Ask your Discipler to answer these questions during your next session. Start by reading Ephesians 1:1-14 during your first daily Quiet Time. Continue reading successive passages. You may wish to break these reading segments into smaller portions by stopping at each new Scriptural insight which you find. May you continue to grow spiritually as you let God mold your character through His Word!

Titus	2 Peter
1:1 - 16	1:1 - 11
2:1 - 15	1:12 - 21
3:1 - 15	2:1 - 12
	2:13 - 22
Philemon	3:1 - 18
1:1 - 25	
	1 John
James	1:1 - 10
1: 1 - 18	2:1 - 14
1:19 - 27	2:15 - 29
2:1 - 13	3:1 - 10
2:14 - 26	3:11 - 24
3:1 - 12	4:1 - 6
3:13 - 18	4:7 - 21
4:1 - 12	5:1 - 12
4:13 - 17	5:13 - 21
5:1 - 12	
5:13 - 20	**2 John**
	1:1 - 13
1 Peter	
1:1 - 12	**3 John**
1:13 - 25	1:1 - 14
2:1 - 12	
2:13 - 25	**Jude**
3:1 - 7	1:1 - 16
3:8 - 22	1:17 - 25
4:1 - 11	
4:12 - 19	
5:1 - 14	

After you have completed these Quiet Time reading segments, you can enjoy reading the rest of the New Testament using the reading schedule on page 88 of your *Spiritual Journal.* Start in Matthew.

"And let us not lose heart in doing good, for in due time we shall reap if we do not grow weary." (Galatians 6:9)

RESOURCE
SECTION

In the United States, please call (800) 880-1350 or FAX (800) 880-8465 for current discounted prices. For U.K. prices and orders, please contact Scripture Union at 041-332-1162, or FAX 041-332-5925.

Spiritual Journals:
Spiritual Journal **Refills** (Classic Edition)
4 Journals per pack

Spiritual Journal **with Suede Jacket** (Classic Edition)
Colors:

Navy	Tan	Gray	Rust
Burgundy	Brown	Dusty Rose	Jade

A Call To Growth:
Discipler's Packet (Word)
Timothy's Packet (Word)

Scripture Memory Packet (Living Word)
52 Scripture verses on color-coded cards covering six topics: New Creations in Christ, Trials and Temptations, Abiding in Christ, Holy Behavior, Spreading the Good News, and Discipleship. Available in NIV, NASB, and KJV.

Victory Scripture Memory Series (Word)
This two booklet system covers the topics of Discipleship
and Spiritual Growth. Each book contains verses for 26
weeks and is available in KJV and NASB.

Steps to Peace with God (Grason) 25 booklets per pack.
Assured of Heaven Cassettes (Word) A direct presentation of the
Gospel on cassette.

Books:

       Everyday Evangelism (Billie Hanks Jr.) (Word)
       If You Love Me (Billie Hanks Jr.) (Word)
       The Gift of Giving (Wayne Watts) (IEA)
       Discipleship (Billie Hanks, Bill Shell) (Zondervan)

Wide Margin Bibles:

NIV - (Cambridge) Page size $7^3/8$" X $8^3/4$"
    $1^1/2$" wide margins for recording insights
    Jesus' words in red
    Double Column Text
    Concordance
    Center Column Cross-References

Color	*Binding*
Black	*Bonded Leather*
Burgundy	*Bonded Leather*

NASB - (Holman) Page Size $6^1/2$" X 9"
    $2^1/4$" wide margins for recording insights
    Jesus' words in red
    Single Column Text
    Concordance
    Side Column References

Color	*Binding*
Black	*Genuine Leather*
Burgundy	*Genuine Leather*
Galilean Blue	*Bonded Leather*
Lydian Purple	*Bonded Leather*

Study Bibles:
NIV - (Zondervan) *The NIV Study Bible*

Color	Binding
Black	Genuine Leather
Burgundy	Genuine Leather
Gray	Genuine Leather
Navy Blue	Genuine Leather
Dusty Rose	Bonded Leather
Forest Green	Bonded Leather

NASB - (Thomas Nelson) *The New Open Bible*

Color	Binding
Black	Genuine Leather
Burgundy	Genuine Leather
Navy Blue	Genuine Leather
Dusty Rose	Bonded Leather
Teal	Bonded Leather

NKJV - (Thomas Nelson) *The New Open Bible*

Color	Binding
Black	Genuine Leather
Burgundy	Genuine Leather
Navy Blue	Genuine Leather
Dusty Rose	Bonded Leather
Teal	Bonded Leather

Exhaustive Concordances:
NIV - (Zondervan) *The NIV Exhaustive Concordance.*
The only exhaustive concordance based on today's most popular Bible. This concordance lists every word in the NIV Bible along with its references. It includes a Hebrew-Aramaic-English index - lexicon, and a Greek-English index-lexicon.

NASB - (Holman) *The NASB Exhaustive Concordance.*
The only exhaustive concordance based on the New
American Standard Bible. Over 400,000 entries list
every word in the NAS Bible along with its references. It includes a Hebrew-Aramaic-English index-
lexicon, and a Greek-English index-lexicon.

INSPIRATIONAL
READING

Chapters
6 – 11

CHAPTER 6

FOLLOW-UP — AN OVERVIEW

Gary W. Kuhne

The first step toward building disciples in our churches begins with follow-up. Brand new Christians or "old" untaught Christians need to be followed-up carefully if they are to achieve the potential for service that God has planned (Ephesians 2:10). Gary W. Kuhne defines follow-up as "the spiritual work of grounding a new believer in the faith." His years of practical experience with Campus and Lay Mobilization in Erie, Pennsylvania, in an evangelistic, follow-up, and discipling ministry, qualify him to speak with authority on this subject. He also served with Campus Crusade for Christ.

Gary Kuhne is a graduate of Pennsylvania State University and at present, is Senior Pastor of Grace Discipleship Church in North East, Pennsylvania.

This chapter, excerpted from his *Dynamics of Personal Follow-up* (Grand Rapids: Zondervan, 1976), deals specifically and practically with the many facets of personal follow-up. Careful study of his material and practical suggestions should motivate us to commit ourselves to personal follow-up.

CHAPTER 6

FOLLOW-UP — AN OVERVIEW

Gary W. Kuhne

"Strengthening the disciples." (Acts 14:22)

For many of you who read this chapter, personal follow-up may be a new concept. It is perhaps a work you have heard about – but you have never actively participated in such a ministry. Don't be ashamed of this. Personal follow-up is simply a ministry that has been neglected by Christian leaders. My experience has shown that the vast majority of people whom I counsel are not personally involved in following up new Christians.

Studies have shown that fewer than one percent of evangelical church members are involved in personal follow-up. For many years, I thought the lack of personal evangelism was one of the greatest problems facing the church. I have not changed my mind as to the seriousness of this problem. But I now believe the lack of effective follow-up being done in the local church today constitutes an even more dangerous problem for the church at large. Perhaps a few examples from my personal experience will show you the reason for my burden in this area.

One of my first exposures to evangelistic outreach began optimistically. A student at Penn State University, I had been a Christian for nearly two years. While in high school, before becoming a Christian, I had been the president of the youth group in my home church, and now I felt a strong burden for the youth currently in that group. I sought to find a way to make the gospel clear to them.

The opportunity presented itself when the youth leader wrote me and requested that I come and lead a weekend retreat. This was a clear answer to prayer, and with the help of several friends, I set about planning the retreat.

The retreat was finally held and God's Spirit moved in a beautiful way. Only one person out of the entire youth group rejected the gospel invitation. I went back to college rejoicing in the Lord. It wasn't long, however, before I began to have serious doubts about the success of that weekend. The youth leader wrote me and told me about problems arising in the group. Several of those who had made commitments were no longer attending. As time went on, all but a few apparently forgot their commitments. I felt helpless to do something about the problem. At that time, I did not see the significant role personal follow-up could have played in conserving the fruit of the retreat. This experience jolted me into discovering how to conserve the fruit of evangelism.

Another situation impressed on me the need for effective personal follow-up. This was an evangelistic film outreach in which I was involved. My role was to act as the head counselor, guiding the work of volunteers who counseled those who came forward in response to the invitation given after the film. The training the counselors received was completely evangelistic in nature, and no attention was given to helping the new believer grow in his new life in Christ (I admit this to my shame). The response in the week of film showings was remarkable. Nearly one thousand people came forward to seek the answer to their needs and problems. After approximately six months, I felt burdened to see what lasting result was evident from our ministry. Although communication was a limiting factor, it was still clear there was little lasting fruit from that project. I could account for fewer than two dozen out of the thousand inquirers who still were going on in their decision. I am not relating this to criticize film evangelism; in fact I feel it is a very effective way to communicate the gospel. I am attempting to show that unless there is a strong emphasis on personal follow-up of decisions, there will be little lasting fruit to show for our efforts.

How much difference can an effective personal follow-up program make in the conservation of fruit in evangelistic outreach? Let me cite another example. An evangelistic church with whose ministry I am acquainted reveals an interesting insight into the role of follow-up in fruit conservation. Examining the church records over the past ten years revealed that approximately six hundred decisions for Christ were made in that time. These decisions resulted from a variety of programs, e.g., youth retreats, evangelism weeks, evangelistic services, and personal evangelism. The profession-of-faith statistics taken from an analysis of membership increase over the same time period numbered less than one hundred. Thus, it would seem that only one out of six decisions was actually conserved. Although this figure does not take into account those who were already members when saved, or those who went on in the Lord and joined some other body, it is safe to say that accurate information concerning these other people would not significantly alter the conservation figure of one out of six.

The reason I chose this church as an example is that the leaders in this church decided they could no longer be content with such a low conservation rate. A number of their people received training in personal follow-up and determined to use their training with every person who would respond to the invitation in their church. Soon after that, they had an evangelistic week at their church and for the first time sought to follow up on all who responded. After six months, the fruit conservation rate was five out of six. Personal follow-up indeed made a significant difference.

My experience over the past several years could multiply these examples of the limitations of evangelism without personal follow-up. Well-planned personal follow-up of new believers could, I am convinced, revolutionize the traditional growth rates of local churches. I believe we can no longer explain away those who don't continue to grow in Christ as being "seeds in bad soil" (see the parable of the sower and the seed in Matthew 13). Undoubtedly, some of those who don't continue to grow in the Lord are the products of "bad soil," yet I see no implication in the text to support a fruit conservation rate of one out of six. Personal experience has shown a much higher rate resulting from effective personal follow-up of new believers. I believe the need is so urgent, we can no longer be complacent about so few lasting results in evangelism.

DEFINITION OF FOLLOW-UP

Since this is a chapter about personal follow-up, it would be good at the outset to define clearly the meaning of this phrase. Because I am unfamiliar with the background of every reader and the meanings he or she applies to terms, it will be necessary for us to establish some common ground in the area of definitions. For the purpose of this chapter, follow-up is defined as follows:

Follow-up is the spiritual work of grounding a new believer in the faith.

This is a generally accepted definition by most Christians I have consulted. The following verses are an example of the emphasis the Bible places on this work of building new believers in the faith.

"We proclaim Him, admonishing and teaching everyone with all wisdom, so that we may present everyone perfect in Christ. To this end I labor, struggling with all His energy, which so powerfully works in me." (Colossians 1:28 & 29)

"They preached the good news in that city and won a large number of disciples. Then they returned to Lystra, Iconium, and Antioch, strengthening the disciples and encouraging them to remain true to the faith." (Acts 14:21 & 22)

In light of the Biblical emphasis on follow-up, the serious Christian has no choice but to do it. The only question that requires discussion is how follow-up can be accomplished most effectively.

An explanation of the basic definition already given is necessary to clarify the content of this term. The spiritual grounding of a new believer in the faith will be the product of both training and teaching. There are certain basic spiritual truths a new Christian must know and apply to become rooted and really begin to grow in Christ. The following is a list of five basic areas of spiritual truth involved in an effective follow-up process:

1. Helping the new believer receive assurance of salvation.
2. Helping the new believer develop a consistent devotional life.
3. Helping the new believer understand the basics of abundant Christian living.
4. Helping the new believer become integrated into the life of a local church.
5. Helping the new believer learn to share his faith with others.

In many respects, follow-up is similar to a parent-child relationship. This is in the spiritual realm, of course. The Bible describes the new believer as a spiritual baby (John 3:3; 1 Corinthians 3:1; 1 Peter 2:2; 1 John 2:12-14). This description is an accurate one. Love, protection, food, and training are all vital spiritual needs that correspond to the physical needs of a baby. As in the physical realm, a new Christian needs a spiritual parent who will watch over him and help provide these necessities during the early stages of his Christian development.

The work of follow-up in a new Christian's life may be better understood by examining the three basic forms it takes: Sunday school group, personal study, and personal follow-up. Group follow-up is that nurturing of the new believer accomplished by the local church or fellowship group. This kind of follow-up takes the form of structured instruction in the basics of doctrine through the use of a new believers' class, Sunday school, or similar program. It also includes the development of committed relationships between the new Christian and the body of believers with whom he associates. The second form, personal study, includes those activities the new Christian engages in on his own. This includes such things as reading books and other literature, and personal Bible study. On both the group and personal study levels of follow-up, there is a good amount of information available to the average pastor and layman to help implement these aspects of a total follow-up ministry. Unfortunately, in the past the same could not be said for the third form, personal follow-up, which is the major emphasis of this chapter. It can be defined as follows:

Personal follow-up is the assuming of a one-to-one relationship by a mature believer with a new Christian for the purpose of aiding the new Christian's nurture and growth.

This type of follow-up, by far the most effective as I will seek to show, is the most neglected form among Christians today.

My experience has shown two major causes for failure in personal follow-up. First, many Christians are unclear as to what needs to be done to help ground a new believer in the faith. In some cases, the Christian has the general knowledge of *what* to say, but is unsure of *how* to say it. This accounts for much ineffectiveness. Second, many Christians are unwilling to give the amount of time that effective personal follow-up requires. Although there are other reasons for the lack of personal follow-up work by Christians, I will focus on these two.

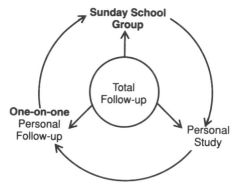

Fig. 1 Elements of a Total Follow-up Program

IMPORTANCE OF PERSONAL FOLLOW-UP

Having clearly dealt with what follow-up is, the question now before us is; Why is personal follow-up important? That the Bible commands us to follow up new believers has already been shown. But since the work of follow-up takes three forms, I would like to propose four reasons why we should not be content to simply abdicate our personal responsibility in follow-up to the group or to the initiative of the new believer, but should rather consider personal follow-up a priority.

1. *The Vulnerability of a New Christian.* A new Christian is more easily deceived by Satan than a more mature Christian. In fact, a new believer is more vulnerable in the fight against Satan's temptations at the beginning of his walk of faith than at any other time of his life. It is common for a new Christian to experience doubt regarding the validity of his decision for Christ. He needs the protection that a more mature believer can help to give him. Victory against Satan's deceptions is to be found only in the truths of God's Word. Christ taught us this by using the Bible to answer Satan's temptations in the wilderness (Matthew 4:1-11; Luke 4:1-13). Knowing little of the Word of God makes a new Christian quite defenseless. This vulnerability is a strong argument for involvement in personal follow-up.

2. *The New Christian's Potential for Change.* A second important reason for personal follow-up involves the new Christian's rate

of growth. A new Christian is at a pivotal point in his life. For the first time, he has the potential for real change in his lifestyle. The direction and guidance offered through personal follow-up greatly increase both the chance and speed of this transformation. Whether one is a young person or an adult, personal follow-up greatly speeds one's growth in Christ. A mature Christian, working in such a close relationship with a new Christian, is able to detect the areas in his life that need the most urgent change. He is also able to assist in the application of pertinent Biblical truth. Without this personal guidance, many new Christians are not able to take full advantage of this crucial period of their lives and do not grow in Christ as rapidly as they could.

A closely related problem is the developing of wrong life patterns in the new Christian who is unsupervised in his growth. These patterns not only hinder his growth, but also present unnecessary sin problems that need to be undone in the future before real, lasting growth can take place. This process of change is described in Scripture as a "putting off" of the old nature and a "putting on" of the new nature. Ephesians 4 and Colossians 3 explain this concept more completely. The truth of these passages should do much to motivate us for the work of personal follow-up.

3. *Disciples Are Produced Most Effectively Through Personal Follow-Up.* A third important reason for doing personal follow-up involves the development of disciples. Personal follow-up greatly increases the speed and probability of discipleship development in a new believer's life. An important and basic goal of your ministry in this area is the development of disciples. It is important that the term *disciple* be clearly defined in our minds. My experience has shown that there are almost as many definitions of this term as there are people. For the purpose of this chapter, a disciple is defined as follows:

A *disciple* is a Christian who is growing in conformity to Christ, is achieving fruit in evangelism, and is working in follow-up to conserve his fruit.

Discipleship training should be a major goal in a total program of personal follow-up. When I use the term *personal follow-up*, I am using it in both a limited and an expanded sense. In the limited sense, I am referring to the initial work of grounding a new believer in the faith. In the expanded sense, I am using the phrase to refer to the entire relationship a mature Christian has with a new Christian over a period of time to help the new Christian achieve maturity. To prevent misunderstanding, I define *discipleship training* as follows:

> *Discipleship training* is the spiritual work of developing spiritual maturity and spiritual reproductiveness in the life of a Christian.

Effective personal follow-up of a new Christian will go far toward conserving more of the fruit of evangelism, but will not in itself speed the fulfillment of the Great Commission. Only an increasing labor force can accomplish this task. The development of spiritual reproductiveness in the new believer's life is the answer to this need. Stated differently, the new Christian must be taught not only to grow in Christ, but also to witness and follow up others who respond to Christ. This alone will achieve a truly multiplying effectiveness in fulfilling the Great Commission. This fact brings us to the fourth reason for making the work of personal follow-up a priority in our life.

4. *Personal Follow-up Is the Most Effective Way of Achieving Spiritual Multiplication.* The degree to which we can encourage a new Christian to be fruit producing has important implications for the fulfillment of the Great Commission. The previous section showed the truth of this statement. Our effectiveness in this work will determine whether we will be spiritual "adders" or "multipliers." Will we only *lead people to Christ,* or will we also be responsible for *their leading others to Christ* (these who in turn will lead others to Christ)? Not only spiritual productiveness, but also spiritual reproductiveness should be the focus of our personal follow-up ministry. To be a multiplier should be the goal of every Christian. A multiplier may be defined as follows:

> A *multiplier* is a disciple who is training his spiritual children to reproduce themselves.

In other words, a multiplier is a disciple who is able to produce other disciples. Only when this process occurs will we see true spiritual multiplication. I define multiplication as follows:

Multiplication is third-generation discipleship training.

To further explain, third-generation discipleship training is seeing someone we have personally discipled, discipling another to disciple others. It is extremely important to understand the concept of spiritual multiplication, for it is the goal of these chapters to produce spiritually multiplying Christians.

Spiritual multiplication is a process that goes through four distinct phases. An explanation of these phases aids in the understanding of this concept.

Phase 1: Evangelizing. The first phase in spiritual multiplication occurs when you share your faith with other people. The command to witness was implied in the Great Commission: *"Therefore go and make disciples of all nations, baptizing them in the name of the Father and of the Son and of the Holy Spirit, and teaching them to obey everything I have commanded you."* (Matthew 28:19 & 20) There can be no short-cut. It is essential that you share Christ with others. Although the *method* of evangelism may vary widely, the *message* cannot. As you share Christ in the power of the Holy Spirit, you will begin to see results, that is, fruit. When an individual repents and receives Christ as his Savior and Lord, you begin the second phase of the multiplication process.

Phase 2: Personal Follow-up. Phase 2 of the multiplication process occurs when you personally start to follow up a new Christian. You begin to meet with him on a regular basis to give him the basic care and teaching he needs to grow in Christ. While in Phase 1, all your ministry time was spent in witnessing; now in Phase 2, you are beginning to devote a growing percentage of your time to the work of building the new Christian. You continue to share Christ even while you are involved in the work of personal follow-up. It is important not to neglect this work. Part of your work in follow-up involves challenging the new believer to a public identification with Christ and a proclaiming of the gospel, that is, witnessing. When the new believer begins to do this, you have in effect doubled your evangelistic outreach as the result of working with another believer to get him involved in witnessing.

It is important to remember that witnessing by itself does not go far enough to fulfill the Great Commission. You must start to train the new Christian to follow up someone else personally (i.e., ground that person in the faith). This is what has been previously defined as discipleship training, or "discipling" for short. When you begin this distinct phase of personal ministry, you begin Phase 3 of the multiplication process.

Phase 3: Discipling. Phase 3 begins when you start to *train* the Christian with whom you are working to personally follow up another new Christian. This occurs when a Christian has grown sufficiently in Christ, or when he leads someone else to Christ. This is a distinct phase, because now you are working with a Christian to enable him not only to keep growing in Christ, but also to become effective in the work of personal follow-up. This adds people not only to the witnessing team, but also to the fruit-conservation team.

The goal is the multiplication of teachers. This is the truth Paul sought to relate to Timothy when he said, *"The things you have heard me say in the presence of many witnesses* [Phase 1] *entrust to reliable men* [Phase 2] *who will also be qualified to teach others* [Phase 3]. *"* (2 Timothy 2:2)

Examine this phase more closely and you will find a great increase in the number of evangelistic contacts. This increase is the product of multiplication of laborers, not the product of increased witnessing on your part. Another significant point comes out when you consider that there are now more people to do follow-up. It is also important to notice that as you go into discipleship training with someone, you will probably see more fruit and start follow-up all over again with someone else.

Phase 4: Multiplying. You probably have a question at this point: Why is there another phase for multiplication? Multiplication really begins when two factors are present:

1. A person has been discipled through Phase 3 (2 Timothy 2:2).
2. This person actually begins to take someone else through a discipling process.

Phase 4 is the multiplying stage of the multiplication process. This is where 2 Timothy 2:2 becomes a reality in your ministry. Phase 4 occurs when a person, followed up and discipled by you, is following up and discipling others. This is the goal of your follow-up ministry and can be accomplished *no other way than through one-to-one involvement and training.* The fulfillment of the Great Commission is a reality only when 2 Timothy 2:2 becomes a reality. We must evangelize, follow up, train, and send if we are to see the world evangelized. If you develop only one truly multiplying disciple each year (not an unreasonable goal), examine the number of evangelistic contacts that will occur as a product of your life over a six-year period. As a result of making a commitment to begin each day by praying for a natural opportunity to witness, let's assume that one evangelistic contact per week is made by each disciple:

Year One
1. Begin year: 1 disciple (you)
2. End year: 2 disciples (you, plus 1)
3. Evangelistic contacts: 50 approximately

Year Two
1. Begin year: 2 disciples
2. End year: 4 disciples
3. Evangelistic contacts: 100 approximately

Year Three
1. Begin year: 4 disciples
2. End year: 8 disciples
3. Evangelistic contacts: 200 approximately

Year Four
1. Begin year: 8 disciples
2. End year: 16 disciples
3. Evangelistic contacts: 400 approximately

Year Five
1. Begin year: 16 disciples
2. End year: 32 disciples
3. Evangelistic contacts: 800 approximately

Year Six
1. Begin year: 32 disciples
2. End year: 64 disciples
3. Evangelistic contacts: 1,600 approximately

In a six-year period, if you disciple only 6 people, you will have caused the eventual development of 64 disciples and the evangelistic confrontation of 1,600 people per year. This is how the multiplication process works. If you continued the process for ten years, you would have personally discipled 10 people and witnessed to 50 a year – but you will have caused the development of 1,024 disciples and the annual confrontation of approximately 25,000 people with the gospel. This isn't just mathematical juggling, but the logical outgrowth of faithful men and women serving the Lord.

The most important "why" of personal follow-up is answered by a firm grasp of the vision of multiplication. My hope is that enough Christians catch this vision to fulfill the Great Commission. A survey of the rapid expansion in world population growth makes the need for multiplication urgently clear.

FACTORS AFFECTING PERSONAL FOLLOW-UP

Personal follow-up, as I have defined and explained it, does not occur in a vacuum and is not entirely free of restraints that inhibit its growth. There are a number of factors that control and regulate the effectiveness of your discipling ministry. Some of these factors are quite obvious and scarcely need mentioning; others are perhaps less obvious and would be important for us to consider and ponder. The following is by no means an exhaustive list of conditions governing an effective personal follow-up ministry, but it is comprehensive and should, if nothing else, stimulate your own evaluation of barriers facing your ministry.

Factor 1: Relationship. Any study of factors affecting a personal follow-up ministry must begin by examining the personal needs of the "discipler." It is important that you be in right relationship with the Lord in your own Christian experience. Personal follow-up is not only methodology, but also life transference. Thus, there can be no substitute for a dynamic relationship with Christ in your own life, if you seek to be effective in helping someone else grow. There will inevitably be a loss of effectiveness if you try to bypass this rule.

Paul clearly focuses on the role of life transference in 1 Thessalonians 2:8: *"We loved you so much that we were delighted to share with you not only the gospel of God but our lives as well, because you had become so dear to us."* A new Christian's growth can be killed in the bud if you focus on methods at the expense of relationship.

Factor 2: Commitment. Multiplication is the product of both personal follow-up and discipleship training, and thus is a time-consuming process. Anything that takes time also takes commitment. Perhaps more than at any other time in history, the average person today is extremely busy. There are many different needs and problems vying for one's attention and involvement. The Christian is not immune to these pressures. In fact, the growing Christian perhaps feels them even more acutely because of the time requirements of church involvement that the non-Christian does not face. With the variety of demands on a Christian (e.g., witnessing, worship services, classes, committees, Bible studies, and prayer meetings), a legitimate question is whether or not the time requirements of personal follow-up are valid in light of projected results.

If an individual begins to do some personal follow-up, he is soon faced with a problem of priorities. There is simply not enough time to do everything. He must soon come to a decision on what his priorities are and, in the light of his priorities, establish what are legitimate activities. I hope the previous discussion of the necessity of multiplication has assisted you in perhaps rethinking priorities. Some necessary questions that need to be asked in your own life are:

"Do I believe in the importance of personal follow-up?"
"Am I willing to spend the time necessary to develop disciples?"
"Am I willing to rethink my present involvements and discontinue those that are no longer a priority?"

Asking questions like these and honestly seeking to answer them will go a long way in causing you to become effective in personal follow-up. Only a committed person is willing to spend the necessary time in follow-up. If you are not totally sold on its importance, as soon as problems and frustrations begin to occur, you will leave to find greener, easier pastures. Commitment plays an important role in the development of effective multiplication.

Factor 3: Concentration. Effective follow-up can never take place if you are attempting to work with too many people at one time. Multiplication depends on spiritually mature and well-trained disciples. This type of disciple is never mass produced, but rather is the product of in-depth, time-consuming, hard work. To achieve true productiveness, you must work with only a few people at a time.

You will need to be totally committed to the concept of personal follow-up to stand against the pressures you are sure to face.

The pressure not to concentrate your energies on a few is going to be great. You may be called selfish and unspiritual, among other things. I remember a pastor who was upset by my insistence on this principle. He told me, "I see that the Bible teaches this idea of concentration, but it is clearly unworkable in the church of today. I have too many responsibilities to concentrate my energies." He was unwilling to adopt the Biblical method because it would mean changing his traditional method of ministry. What a tragedy!

It is important that you withstand this pressure. This will be possible only if you have a long-range view of your ministry and are not tyrannized by the urgent needs around you. Early in His ministry, Christ chose a core of men and began to pour His life into them. His purpose was to create the leadership necessary to oversee the growth of the early church adequately. In a real sense, Christ staked His entire future effectiveness on these few men. He did not misread God's will in this matter. Under the empowerment of the Holy Spirit, these disciples multiplied, taking the gospel to Jerusalem, Judea, Samaria, and the world (Acts 1:8).

Perhaps the diagram on the following page will be helpful in illustrating the concentration technique employed by Christ. Starting with Christ at the center, the time spent varies inversely with the distance from the center.

Waylon Moore, in his book *New Testament Follow-up* (Grand Rapids: Eerdmans, 1963), discusses various laws governing multiplication. One of the most important is the factor of concentration. He states, "A decision that our ministry will be intensive, rather than extensive will change our whole life. Quality begets quantity. It takes vision to train one man to reach the masses." (p. 68) There is no substitute for the role of personal discipleship development, and this can occur only when we concentrate our energies.

Factor 4: Duration. Christ poured three years of His life into the twelve apostles. Near the end of this time (approximately six months), He spent nearly all of His time with them. Thus Christ, the master Discipler, felt it necessary to do this to ensure the massive multiplication of the Christian church over the following quarter of a century. *If there had been a better way, Christ would have used it.* You would not have been very impressed if you had been an uninvolved bystander at that period of time. There were not more than five hundred followers at the time of Christ's death, and many of these were only peripherally involved. Yet Christ was satisfied with His work, for He saw in His disciples the future multiplication of the church.

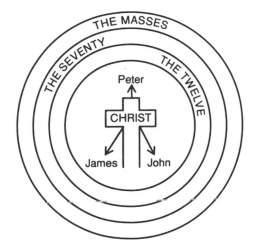

**Fig. 2. The Principle of Concentration
in the Ministry of Christ**

Waylon Moore stresses this principle and its application to the encouragement of discipleship. He states that it takes multiplication approximately three to five years to become obvious (p. 69). This means it takes that long before people become aware of the growth in their midst. Many laymen and pastors are afflicted with a spiritual shortsightedness. They do not seem to notice the groundwork laid for a ministry process over a period of years, but rather they see only what you are currently doing to achieve growth. This explains why so many have missed the truth of multiplication for so long.

CHAPTER 7

DEVELOPING A MEANINGFUL RELATIONSHIP

Gary W. Kuhne

"A friend loves at all times." (Proverbs 17:17)

Developing a close friendship with a new believer is a basic ingredient in effectively following up a new Christian, for it involves a nurturing that goes beyond merely the teaching and enforcing of rules. It also involves a loving communication of those rules, and a loving communication of a life.

When I first attempted follow-up, I had a difficult time developing relationships with new Christians. The problem was my approach. I was assuming that relationships just naturally occur. In some cases they may, especially if the individual has some areas of interest in common with you. Unfortunately, in personal follow-up you will often be working with someone with whom you have little in common. In this circumstance, it will take concerted effort to build an effective relationship. Over time, I discovered a variety of "tools" for building relationships. Along with these came a thrilling sense of spiritual victory in my own life. No longer was I limited to certain types of people for effectiveness in my ministry. I have found a similar joyous response in people I have trained in follow-up ministry. In Christ, there is truly neither slave nor free, Jew nor Greek.

Spiritual parenthood has many of the same characteristics as physical parenthood. How many of us could be content merely to be a rule-giver and enforcer with our children? In addition to being an authority figure, a good parent is constantly seeking to know his children better and develop a good relationship with them. This

137

is also true when it comes to following up a new Christian effectively. We do need to be authority figures, that is, spiritual leaders
who communicate the how-to's of growing in Christ. At the same
time however, we must also be developing meaningful relationships
with new Christians. The purpose of this chapter is to offer some
practical advice on developing this relationship with a new Christian.

DEVELOP AN ATMOSPHERE OF LOVING CONCERN

One of the first ways to begin developing a meaningful relationship with a new Christian is by being honestly concerned for him,
really wanting to be his friend. *"A friend loves at all times, and
a brother is born for adversity."* (Proverbs 17:17) Paul clearly
teaches this as one of the important elements in his own follow-up
ministry. For example, examine the way Paul described his attitude toward the Philippians: *"God can testify how I long for all of
you with the affection of Christ Jesus."* (Philippians 1:8) He begins
by saying, *"God can testify."* It is important to understand why he
starts this way. Paul doesn't use this term lightly, but rather uses it
only when he wants to make something unquestionably clear to us.
When he said, *"God can testify,"* Paul knew he was calling an om-
niscient God to witness to the truth of his statement.

This was necessary because of what Paul went on to claim about
the way he felt toward them: *"God can testify how I long for all of
you with the affection of Christ Jesus."* What a statement! This
describes the point I am trying to make. How much do you really
care about the people you are following up? Do you love them
with the affection of Christ? If you do, the relationship is bound to
develop; if you don't, the relationship will be hindered. We need to
build into our lives the attitude that enables us to say with Paul,
"God is my witness" (RSV), I'm burdened over that new Christian.

I remember working with a young married student. Although I
worked hard, I seemed to be getting nowhere in my follow-up. I
was unable to gain his confidence, and our relationship was a shallow one. One day while thinking about the problem, it occurred to
me that I really didn't care about the fellow. I wasn't burdened for
his growth, but rather was slightly irritated at the trouble he was
causing me. What a sobering and convicting discovery this was. I
determined to begin to focus my prayers and concern on him as a
person, and to seek to develop the love God desired me to have for

him as an individual. It wasn't long before there were some real breakthroughs in follow-up. That young man is now serving God effectively in vocational Christian service.

Do you genuinely want to help the new Christian grow in Christ? Do you honestly care about people? If you feel you need more love and concern to answer in the affirmative, you can pray and specifically ask God to develop that kind of attitude in your life. Through prayer, God will give you this type of burden. The Bible doesn't explain why the mechanics of prayer work this way, but there is something about interceding for a person that increases your burden for him.

Pray for specific things. If you run out of things to pray for, start reading the first part of many of Paul's epistles. There, he makes specific prayers for spiritual growth on the part of the new believers. In your prayers, insert the name of the person you are following up. If over a period of time you keep praying for him in a disciplined way, God will develop that burden within your heart. You probably won't notice it grow, yet soon you will find yourself sincerely caring for that individual.

There is one exciting implication of this truth I want to emphasize. You can feel a burden for, and thus build a relationship with someone you would not naturally choose for a friend. When I was in college, I had a pastor who helped me a great deal in my own Christian growth and thinking. Once he said something I will never forget: "Before you became a Christian, you picked out your friends. After you became a Christian, God began to pick out your friends, and often He picks out people you never would." When you are paired into relationships with Christians whom you would never choose to be your friends, it forces you to turn to God for the strength and love you need to develop the relationships. In personal follow-up, you can't pick and choose who is going to respond to Christ. Sooner or later you are going to find yourself in personal follow-up relationships with people you would not normally choose to spend time with. God can work around that problem. He can *give* you the attitude you need to develop a friendship with those people.

When you are seeking to build friendships with new Christians, it is important that you have an accepting kind of love. Jesus applied this principle of accepting love as He worked with His disciples. His love and concern for those disciples were basic tools in their spiritual growth. They knew He loved them; there was never any doubt in their minds. Even when they failed, the atmosphere was one of concerned acceptance. The Lord rebuked them when they failed, but He still loved them and continued to work with them, helping them to learn from their mistakes. In spite of their failures, they knew Christ's love was unconditional.

An important question to ponder is whether you are creating or will create this kind of environment or atmosphere of unconditional acceptance and love for a person. Please don't misunderstand. This doesn't imply overlooking people's sinfulness, but rather it means accepting them in the face of their failings and showing them how to deal with any problems they have. You can love them and help them discover God's way out of it. It is possible to accept the person and at the same time not accept the sinful shortcomings in his or her life. As you work with people, do you create that kind of accepting atmosphere?

A good way to test yourself is to check out why the new Christian does what you assign him. Is it the result of his motivation to grow in Christ – or is he afraid that if he slips up, you will reject him? Is he performing for your sake, or the Lord's? When pleasing you is the exclusive motivation in a new believer's life, there is something seriously wrong. It's going to be extremely difficult to develop in that person the proper kind of motivation. Are you creating the kind of an atmosphere of love that is helping to motivate the new Christian to grow?

DEVELOP YOUR RELATIONSHIP AROUND CHRIST

A second major truth in building relationships is to develop your relationship around Christ. It is important to realize that this will take real effort, because the natural thing is to try to develop a relationship around something else. You develop a relationship with one person because he likes basketball, with another because he likes art. Having things in common is a good aid in developing a relationship, but when it becomes the center or focus of your relationship, you become limited in your circle of friends. John gives us the correct focus for lasting relationships: *"We proclaim to you what we have seen and heard, so that you also may have fellowship with us. And our fellowship is with the Father and with His Son, Jesus Christ."* (1 John 1:3)

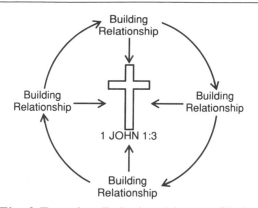

Fig. 3 Focusing Relationships on Christ

John declares that Christ is the focal point of true fellowship. He claims that relationships should be developed around knowing Christ. This does not mean it is wrong to have other things in common with a person you are following up. What it does mean is that often you are going to be put in a follow-up relationship with someone with whom you have little in common. This should not prevent you from having a meaningful relationship and friendship if Christ is at the center.

How do you make Christ the focus? From the very beginning of follow-up with a new Christian, spend the bulk of your time on spiritual things. This doesn't mean lecturing that person, but it does mean devoting most of your time to spiritual communication, creating an atmosphere of spiritual sharing. Make it a natural thing to share with each other what God is doing and what God is teaching you through His Word. This develops naturally only when it is the way you act in the initial stages of that relationship. If you develop your relationship around something else, you will have to force Christ-centered discussion, and it becomes an awkward unnatural thing. If you develop your relationship from the beginning around Christ and spiritual things, the pattern is set for future openness.

There is another important factor in developing your relationship around Christ. Whenever you are with a new Christian, strive formally or informally to talk about something spiritual. Since formal sharing and teaching occur naturally when you meet for a follow-up session, there is no need to elaborate on the formal aspect of this truth. But let me give you a few examples of what I mean by informal sharing:

One tool you can use to develop a relationship with a new Christian is a common interest in baseball. Going to a ball game is a secular activity used for developing relationships. Even in the midst of a game, you can be teaching. I know of one person who used such a setting to tell about one of the ways God made a distinct change in his life in the area of attitudes. When he played baseball in school, he was aggressively involved in the game. This attitude carried over when he became a spectator. His aggressiveness would express itself beyond yelling and cheering. He also verbally assaulted various referees he didn't think were doing a good job. His attitude was sinful. But God changed him and gave him victory over the problem. By sharing this with the new Christian, he was able to show in a practical way how God makes a difference in the Christian's life. This is a good example of communicating a spiritual truth informally. It may not have been an ideal teaching environment, yet informally he was communicating a deep spiritual truth to that new Christian.

Another example of this informal teaching might involve two people who go shopping together as a tool for developing their relationship. Perhaps there are many others around, and it is hectic. This is a perfect opportunity to relate how you used to get frustrated and uptight in this kind of situation, but God has given you patience and peace to keep a good witness for Him in the face of adverse circumstances (Philippians 4:10-13). If God hasn't done that work in you yet, it will be impossible to share in this way, and you shouldn't lie about it. However, this example should make the point clear to you that even in secular situations, you can have an informal time of sharing. You ought to be communicating something positive continually.

When I started training my first disciples, I made it a rule never to meet with someone for follow-up or discipleship unless I had something fresh to give him. I wanted to talk about something new God had taught me or reinforced in my mind during my personal study of the Word. As God has given me strength, I have never since that time failed to communicate a fresh spiritual truth when I met someone for follow-up. You don't have to keep reaching back into your memory. If you are in the Word, the Lord gives you something constructive every time. It may not be a brand-new insight; it can be a reinforcement of a truth you already know. You can always communicate this kind of truth. This is the best way to get the new Christian to the point where he will begin to share with you, too.

A question at this point might be how to motivate people to study the Word. The best way to motivate a new Christian toward Bible study is to use the Bible when you deal with his problems and tell how you use it when you are solving your own problems. Jesus motivated His followers to use the Word mainly because *He* used it. In answer to their questions and problems, Jesus quoted the Old Testament 160 times in the presence of His disciples. That is how you motivate people to study the Word.

PERSEVERANCE

The next important factor in developing relationships with new believers involves the ingredient of perseverance, or patience. It takes time to build relationships. The new Christian's relationship with God is going to take time to develop, and it is also going to take time for that new Christian's relationship with you to grow. Friendships will not always grow smoothly, or even at the same rate. Sometimes a new Christian may not seem to be responding at all, yet you need to stick with him.

The fact that a person isn't growing at a certain rate or always being victorious over sin should not discourage you. A person may stumble one week and the next week be renewed from the Word, getting back on the right track once more. Although discouraging, these periods of defeat are not disastrous for one's overall Christian life. This is especially true if one learns from his failures. Learn to have patience in the face of failures. Everyone falls down once in a while, and the new Christian you are following up is no exception.

Do not take it personally when the new Christian stumbles. I often find that this problem arises among those doing personal follow-up. In other words, you will sometimes be tempted to take the new Christian's stumbling as a reflection on your "follow-up expertise." How dare he fail after you did such a good job communicating how not to fail! Of course, sometimes we need to become upset. This motivates us to help our young Christian friend deal with his problems. But when we become upset because our feelings are hurt and our pride is trampled on, then we are sinning. Our main concern should be that the sin is hurting the new Christian's growth.

We also need patience to discern the new Christian's attitude in the midst of the failure. Is he repentant, wanting to learn from his mistake, or is he rebellious? It is important that you have discernment at this point. Attitudes at times are not clearly reflected by actions. This is true because actions, in many cases, are controlled by both the past and the present environments of the person. It takes patience and discernment to discover the inner attitude of the new Christian. But you *can* find it because God reveals it to you. It is difficult to detect attitude problems if you don't know what is happening inside an individual. Although you won't totally understand a person's problems and attitudes, you do have the leading of the Holy Spirit to give you a sensitivity others lack.

In his encounter with Ananias and Sapphira (Acts 5), Peter gives us a perfect example of this sensitivity. He was able to see beneath the surface of the problem by detecting wrong attitudes. This example also shows there may be sinful attitudes present even in the right kind of actions. Only in Christ is it possible to gain this type of insight.

Another important element of perseverance is being willing to reprove the new Christian when he needs reproof. Whenever he stumbles, it is important that he deal with his problem. In other words, confront him with his sin and then show him how to solve the problem and get back into a right relationship with God. The idea here is to use both the corrective and rebuking aspects of the Word of God as they are revealed in 2 Timothy 3:16 & 17.

SPEND QUALITY TIME TOGETHER

"There are friends who pretend to be friends, but there is a friend who sticks closer than a brother." (Proverbs 18:24 RSV) The next factor to consider in developing relationships is the role of association. By association I mean spending time with the new Christian. It is somewhat easier for the association to take place in youth work than in adult work, since an adult's time is much more rigidly structured by family responsibilities and similar restrictions. Yet, in spite of the difficulty involved in finding time to spend with an adult who is a new believer, it is still necessary that we do so. For instance, homemakers may be able to meet over mid-morning coffee, those in business over lunch. Choose an optimal time for both of you.

When seeking to find activities that aid association, look for something you are already doing to which you could invite the new

Christian. This is the key to finding time to do effective personal follow-up. By doing two things at once, you squeeze extra hours into a twenty-four-hour day. It is possible to piggy-back your time to aid you in association.

One example of how to accomplish this is to take the new Christian with you when you go to church. The reason you take him with you is not simply to get him to go to church, although that is one reason. It is also for that twenty minutes driving home when you can discuss the sermon. The important thing is just spending time talking together and fellowshipping. We can each find some way to spend time with a new Christian. It may take some effort, but the real problem is one of burden, not time.

Spending time with the new believer is the essence of a truly effective follow-up program. I hope this list of examples will stimulate your own thinking.

1. Going to church
2. Short trips
3. Shopping
4. Going to sporting events
5. Camping
6. Picnics
7. Holiday activities
8. Washing your cars

A new Christian often becomes most open and honest about his victories, defeats, and problems in the informal times. Do all you can to create these all-important times of informal fellowship with a new believer.

MINISTER TO THE TOTAL PERSON

The next factor conditioning the development of effective relationships with new Christians concerns the problem of viewing our role from too limited a perspective. We can sometimes become overly concerned about the spiritual side of a person's life and neglect other aspects involved. Each individual is made up of many interrelated parts that form a single whole. The spiritual affects the social, and the social can also affect the spiritual. This interrelatedness is found in every area of a person's life, and because of this, you have to deal with more than the spiritual needs of a new Christian.

For example, let's consider the possible relationship between a social problem and a spiritual need in a new believer. An important aspect of personal follow-up is getting the new believer into good

Christian fellowship. What will happen if the person you are following up has some social problems that limit his ability to develop good relationships with other Christians? It is obvious that his social problems will cause some spiritual problems as time goes by. It is, therefore, important that you are able to detect and deal with social problems as one step to seeing real growth in a person's life.

Let's pursue this example further. The new Christian with whom you are working has a problem that is socially restricting. Your purpose in helping him with this problem is not so much to develop a well-polished individual, but rather to help him develop qualities to aid him in having fellowship with other Christians. There are various ways to help someone who is shy. If you have had this problem, show the new Christian what God has revealed to you from His Word to help you deal with it. Just to sit down with him in a follow-up visit and tell him he must get to know people and that God doesn't want him to be shy won't usually solve the problem. It is much more effective to show the new Christian how to do something about his problem and help him actually encounter other people.

Perhaps the person you are following up is blunt or loud or turns others off. The best thing to do is to sit down with him and tell him his behavior offends other people. Often a person doesn't realize the reaction of others toward his behavior. He has developed a certain manner of social behavior, not realizing how it bothers other people. You might also work out some prearranged signal to tell the person when he is becoming offensive, or when he is saying something that should not be said. You do not need to be an expert on social graces to help the new Christian relate to the group.

Perhaps the new Christian needs counseling on family problems. I remember the home situation of one teenager I was following up. The father came home drunk every night and beat up the family. Obviously you need to do more than just go over follow-up appointments with such a person. To begin helping a new Christian, you must get to know more about the circumstances he faces. In this case, the new Christian had neglected his devotions. It turned out he wanted to take time for them, but because of the family situation at home, he was unable to do so. If I had kept urging him to have devotions without seeking to help this complicated problem, I would only have succeeded in creating frustration and wide communication gaps.

Perhaps the person you are working with has hygiene problems. Who is going to tell him if you don't? You should work toward developing the type of relationship with him that will enable you to give guidance in areas that otherwise might have been embarrassing. Your purpose is not to pry, but rather to help him grow in Christ. You are trying to help him become a confident individual. I'm not advocating that you inquire into areas where you are not wanted. Don't force a person to tell you everything. Just be open and receptive. All of this will contribute to developing an attitude of acceptance and mutual confidence, which will greatly aid you in the area of spiritual follow-up. As the new Christian develops confidence in you, he is going to believe more and more of what you say and accept it as authority. This is especially true when it comes to solving problems.

Perhaps the new Christian has a financial difficulty. Maybe his problem is an unworkable budget since many people just don't know how to make a good budget. Bitter experience taught me how to budget. Perhaps he is going through all kinds of struggle and worry as a result of this problem. To sit down and talk to him about worry will not help him if you can't get to the root of his problem. Again, the point here is the need to see each individual as a total person, and not just address yourself to one segment of his life.

REMEMBER WHAT HE TELLS YOU

Another factor in developing relationships is to remember what the new Christian shares with you. Both as a student and as a vocational Christian worker, I had some bitter experiences in this area. I had a habit of forgetting what people told me. There were times when I met with someone and would forget what his major was in college or what courses he was taking. This can really become embarrassing. People begin to think you don't really care.

After being embarrassed several times, I developed an easy method of storing information that really helped me with this problem. I began to carry a 3 x 5 card to fill out after I finished meeting with a person. I would jot down all the important information he had told me. Before the next time we met, I reviewed the 3 x 5 card. In the initial stages of working with a person, it is extremely important to have that information. I mention this problem because it has happened to me and it may well happen to you. If you have a bad memory, start writing things down.

BE A LEADER AS WELL AS A FRIEND

The next factor in developing a relationship with a new Christian is the need to strike the right balance between being both spiritual leader and friend. In the midst of today's emphasis on friendship and relationship, it is easy to sidestep being a leader. None of us really wants the responsibility of being a leader. We would much rather avoid having to help a new Christian grow in Christ. We prefer to sidestep our responsibility to confront a new believer involved in a sin; we try to put all the responsibility on the Lord to reprove and convict him. This takes the pressure away from us. It is much easier, but much less effective to remain nonauthoritative in our relationship.

This is one side of the coin. It is also important to realize that it is possible to become too authoritative or problem-oriented. It is best to deal with only one problem at a time, which is quite enough to keep a person busy. Be careful not to make your whole relationship one of constantly telling the new Christian what he did wrong. It is much better to have a healthy balance in your relationship of mutual encouragement, sharing of spiritual truths, and counseling. If you keep it balanced, you won't create a negative atmosphere of defeat and legalism.

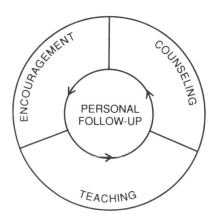

Fig. 4 Keeping Balance in Follow-Up

You won't always get positive responses from the new Christian as you attempt to be his spiritual leader. There will be negative reactions to deal with as well. You must show him that negative reactions are sinful. If you have been presenting the Word of God to point out a particular problem, and he rebels against it, his rebellion is not against you, but against God's will. If however, you have been obnoxious or tried to push too many things on him at one time, then his reaction is your fault. Achieving a good balance is essential.

Another important element in being an effective leader is to deal with problems when they arise and in the order of their priority. There may be more than one obvious problem at a particular time. Deal with the one most crucial to his spiritual growth. If you will deal with problems when they first arise, you keep them from becoming major. This honest dealing with problems helps the new Christian develop good habits of Christian living. If however, you wait too long to deal with a problem, the new Christian will have developed a bad habit. When this happens, the problem becomes harder to deal with and overcome. I am convinced problem-solving is a crucial part of follow-up and discipleship. I hope you will begin to see that it does play and important role and that you are called to be a spiritual leader who gives direction to people in solving their problems. Ask God to help you be an effective friend and leader to the new Christian He has entrusted into your care.

CHAPTER 8

A NEW TESTAMENT
APPROACH TO MINISTRY

Billie Hanks, Jr.

The whole process of discipleship and disciple-making begins with a vision. We have to see first of all, that discipleship is the kind of life God expects of us as Christians. We are called to be followers of Jesus Christ – disciples. But we are also mandated to *"go and make disciples,"* which is disciple-making or the multiplying of disciples. And we begin by developing a Biblical vision for both.

Billie Hanks Jr., has been a practitioner of these concepts for years and is an experienced disciple-maker. Through reading Dawson Trotman's *Born to Reproduce* booklet, Hanks caught the vision for spiritual multiplication, developed it into a well-honed curriculum for the local church, and has been training pastors and lay leaders on how to have and multiply a thriving discipleship ministry in the church.

Dr. Hanks is President of International Evangelism Association based in Salado, Texas, and has visited more than sixty countries in the course of his evangelistic and disciple-making ministry. He also heads a discipleship training center for collegiate and seminary men and women. This ministry is located at West Texas Ranch for Christ near Sweetwater, Texas. He holds degrees from Baylor University and Southwestern Baptist Theological Seminary.

Along with his preaching and training ministry, Hanks composes sacred hymns and folk songs. His popular ballad "Lonely Voices" has been a religious music best seller known around the world.

A NEW TESTAMENT APPROACH TO MINISTRY

Billie Hanks, Jr.

"And this gospel of the kingdom will be preached in the whole world as a testimony to all nations, and then the end will come."
(Matthew 24:14)

On a sunny Florida afternoon years ago, I heard the haunting and unforgettable words of a leading evangelical British minister who said, "Mark my words, North American Christians: Your large church buildings will be as empty as the cathedrals of Great Britain within a span of twenty-five to fifty years if you do not change your methodology."

The well-known cleric spoke with the assurance of a prophet, yet the humility of one who had been mellowed by many years of Christian service.

OUR TRADITIONAL METHODOLOGY

After hearing the English pastor speak, I decided to investigate his claims. In subsequent years, I spent considerable time in Great Britain and Europe and learned to appreciate the wisdom of his words. I discovered striking similarities between the declining spiritual vitality of church members in Great Britain decades ago, and what we are currently seeing in large segments of the church in other parts of the world. The methodology he spoke about had to do with how we assimilate, nurture, and train our new church members. His earnest warning calls us to reexamine the way we do our follow-up and evangelism.

One day while I was working in a Billy Graham crusade in London, I was invited to lunch by one of England's leading young Anglican evangelists. Over the meal, we discussed evangelism in our two countries and compared our various methods and approaches to ministry.

After graciously complimenting my denomination for being one of the world's most evangelistic, he asked me a penetrating question: "What percentage of your laity normally lead someone else to Jesus Christ during any given year?"

I was embarrassed to tell him that even in our best years, fewer than 5 percent of our laity and clergy *combined* lead anyone to a saving knowledge of Christ. I went on to explain that in North America, we have an army of good people who are sympathetic with evangelism, however, only a small percentage of them actually witness. As a result, a few are doing the work of many.

Consciously or unconsciously, churches are actually wasting their most valuable resource for personal evangelism. They don't seem to realize that most new Christians sincerely *desire* to grow and serve the Lord. They also have a host of lost friends! Unfortunately however, most of these friends remain lost simply because the new members are not followed up and shown how to study the Bible, pray, or effectively share the gospel.

Because of this unattended problem, a high percentage of an average congregation is often inactive, and many church members cannot even be found. Obviously, new converts who seldom attend church and never really grow will also miss the joy of winning and training others for Christ. For this reason, it needs to be clearly stated that evangelism's most persistent enemy is poorly planned and poorly executed follow-up.

THE EVANGELIZED AS EVANGELIZERS

The real issue involved in new member assimilation is international in scope. Few questions are as critical to the future of the church. The challenge of educating, inspiring, and equipping today's generation of new members is far reaching. This task is much larger than any single denomination, organization, or program can accomplish alone. Something of this magnitude requires the joint prayers and efforts of all Christians. It calls us to return to the Biblical principles modeled by the early church.

This need is urgent because the methods inherited from recent tradition are simply not working in terms of the Great Commission. We can clearly see that once-Christian parts of the world now desperately need to be re-evangelized. History has taught us that numerical growth by occasional addition is totally inadequate to keep up with the global biological birthrate.

For this reason, we must take strategic steps to ensure that the new Christians of our day are equipped to become strong reproducing witnesses. Through our care, example, and encouragement, they can go much further than past generations. They can build lasting ministries of spiritual multiplication! Dr. Herschel H. Hobbs has wisely said, "The work of evangelism is never complete until the one evangelized becomes an evangelizer." Amplifying this statement, if the process of making disciples is to be complete, all new Christians should be mentored and shown how to explain and defend their faith. This full-circle of apprenticeship takes time. It also requires love, discipline, and personal commitment. However, you will discover that the added work in personal follow-up is well worth the investment, because it produces spiritual fruit that remains and multiplies.

Because we have the Lord's promise, we know that the church's great evangelistic task will definitely be carried out (Matthew 24:14). But the time has come to update our methodology so we will be operating on the principles revealed in Christ's ministry. This will be explained more fully in the next chapter by Dr. Robert Coleman. The Gospels reveal that Jesus trained His disciples by association long before giving them the Great Commission. Being *with* Him was their primary means of learning how to minister. Mark tells us, *"He appointed twelve – designating them apostles – that they might be with Him and that He might send them out to preach."* (Mark 3:14) This same principle was echoed by Paul in 1 Corinthians 11:1, *"Follow my example, as I follow the example of Christ."*

The early disciples' understanding of evangelism grew out of a lifestyle seasoned by many hours in Jesus' presence. They were apprenticed in real-life situations. They saw evangelism, counseling, preaching, teaching, and every other form of ministry firsthand. Jesus' pattern for training was both simple and successful, *"Come, follow Me and I will make you fishers of men."* (Matthew 4:19) He showed them how to minister by simply letting them watch Him do it!

YOUR MINISTRY

As a Discipler in your own church, you will enjoy Christ-centered friendships that focus upon two principle ministries. Both of these ministries were carried out by Jesus and emulated by the apostles. Paul said, *"All that you heard me say, (teaching) and saw me do, (training) put into practice and the God of peace will be with you."* (Philippians 4:9) One of your ministries will be teaching, and the other will be training. Both are essential in a new member's process of growth.

The Biblical preaching provided by your pastor is vital because it builds a new member's faith (Romans 10:17). However, a church's public ministry should be enhanced by it's private ministry. We can see this modeled in the Lord's example. His leadership instruction was most often given while alone with His men. In private, they felt free to ask their questions without any fear of embarrassment. Through experience, you will probably discover the benefit of this same principle.

The critical need for most churches is restored balance! This means enjoying corporate worship and small group Bible study, but it also means reestablishing the New Testament pattern of personal apprenticeship. Said simply, a church needs three basic ministries: one-to-one, one-to-some, and one-to-many.

Under mature spiritual leadership committed to this balanced approach, today's new church members can be taught and shown how to carry out their God-given ministries (see Ephesians 2:10). When this takes place, steady evangelistic growth will begin to take place naturally through the power of spiritual multiplication. In time, the average believer will experience the "joy" of personally leading others to Christ!

TAKING GOD'S MANDATE SERIOUSLY

"And the things which you have heard from me in the presence of many witnesses, these entrust to faithful men, who will be able to teach others also." (2 Timothy 2:2, NASB)

Billy Graham has said:
"2 Timothy 2:2 is a little like a mathematical formula for spreading the gospel and enlarging the church. Paul taught

Timothy; Timothy shared what he knew with faithful men; these faithful men would then teach others also. And so the process goes on and on. If every believer followed this pattern, the church could reach the entire world with the gospel in one generation! Mass crusades in which I believe and to which I have committed my life, will never finish the Great Commission; but a one-by-one ministry will." (The Holy Spirit, Waco: Word, 1978, p. 147)

As an evangelist, I am in deep agreement with Dr. Graham that evangelism, by addition alone, will never reach the world for Christ. This is why the guiding principle behind *A Call to Joy* is spiritual multiplication. It is the first step on a journey, and it lays the foundation for a lifestyle of winning and discipling one person at a time. Why is this important? Because the Lord's plan involves everyone as His witness (Acts 1:8). Only by this simple, personal approach, do we have the realistic potential of reaching every nation with the gospel.

Neglecting this relational form of ministry ultimately produces a deep sense of frustration and spiritual fatigue in the lives of sincere Christian people. As believers, we can find ourselves absorbed in a host of mundane activities and actually miss the vitality and fulfillment of feeding and leading the Lord's lambs and sheep.

Over a period of time, the lack of personal ministry and good discipleship training can leave a church without a strong base of qualified lay leadership. As a result, a church staff may find itself carrying out the ministries of counseling, hospital visitation, and evangelistic ministries largely on their own. This of course is unbiblical and unproductive.

When we feel that our time has become too valuable for us to personally equip the new members, we are actually forfeiting some of the church's future spiritual leaders. When that happens, the vicious cycle simply repeats itself again! In vivid contrast, the Lord revealed His own pattern of ministry by investing His maximum time in the lives of those who would bear the maximum responsibility for the future ministry of the church. For Him, leadership training began almost immediately after He met each new disciple who would some day be an apostle. Spiritual nurture and equipping was blended together to produce godly men with great strength and maturity.

FOLLOWING JESUS' EXAMPLE

One morning, I received a long-distance phone call from a friend who pastored the largest church in his county. After three years of ministry there, he was discouraged and wanted to move on to another church field, so he asked me to pray with him about the matter.

I asked whether he had ever tried investing a portion of his time in the lives of some of his key laymen. He replied, "I don't have one layman who would be interested."

I told him I felt sure that in a congregation of five hundred, there must be several people who would respond to the challenge of personal training in spiritual growth and evangelism. I then asked him why he wanted to leave.

"My people are not spiritual," he replied. "Sunday attendance fluctuates with the weather and our Sunday school teachers are so irresponsible they do not even notify their classes when they are planning to miss."

"If that is a justification for leaving a church," I told him, "half the pastors in America would have reason to resign." I challenged him again to start looking for faithful future leaders to train.

Six weeks later he called a second time. His enthusiasm was electric! He literally shouted over the phone, "Billie, praise God, I've found three men! I am meeting with one on Mondays, another on Tuesdays, and with the third on Thursday."

"Do you still want me to recommend you to another church?" I asked.

"Definitely not!" he replied. "You couldn't move me out of this town with a crowbar!"

As we talked, I discovered that Sunday school had not changed, church attendance still fluctuated, and overall the circumstances were pretty much the same as before. What had changed? Three men were now meeting with God for a daily quiet time, memorizing Scripture, forming new priorities in their lives, and beginning to share their faith naturally.

My friend was exuberant because he was now being fulfilled through what was happening in the lives of only three men. Their growth marked the beginning of a bright new era in his life. Through this one experience, he learned a new way of investing his time, and soon he was following Jesus' example!

THE PRINCIPLE APPLIED

If a new member fails to establish a friendship which models personal spiritual growth and evangelism, he will ultimately settle into a life of churchmanship, rather than effective ministry. In many instances, he will also be left wide open to an assortment of false doctrines. Tragically, he may even be victimized by movements that thrive on well-meaning, but immature new believers. Why? Because he failed to receive the guidance, instruction, and caring friendship of a more mature Christian.

Isn't it time for us to rediscover the art of simply being with people? We need to befriend them like Barnabas, and pray for them like Paul (Acts 14:21-23). Then, our generation can expect to see the greatest multiplication of converts since the early days of the Christian church. Through the first century believers, we have already been shown the strategy for success (2 Timothy 2:2).

For application, let's visualize one solitary Christian seeking to evangelize an entire community – can it be done? It might take a full year of prayer and witnessing to reach the first person for Christ. It might even take another full year for the two Christians to each reach and train another. Does this process seem slow? At first glance, it might appear so, but if this chain of multiplication remains unbroken for just 20 years, an entire city of more than one million people can be evangelized!

As a Discipler, you can have a vital role in reaching your neighborhood, city, and world for Christ, because you will be serving on the front lines in terms of ministry.

Our critical times call for new vision and a return to a fully absorbed philosophy of ministry. We must harness the power of evangelistic multiplication and commit ourselves to the long-range strategy of equipping all the Lord's people to be spiritual reproducers. No new or existing member in your church can be overlooked because they each have a calling, God given gifts, and great potential.

As you prepare to serve as a Discipler, you will have the Word of God, the Holy Spirit, and the privilege of prayer as your resources. So be encouraged by this promise, *"...faithful is the One who calls you, who will also do it."* (1 Thessalonians 5:24)

ASSOCIATION WITH JESUS

Robert E. Coleman

How do we get started? The answer to this is another question – How did Jesus do it? His methodology was to spend quality time with His disciples, pouring His life into theirs. To do this, He had to be with them, and this is the concept of association.

Robert Coleman discusses the Biblical basis for the ministry of association in the second chapter of *The Master Plan of Evangelism*, presented here as chapter 9. Jesus had a thriving public ministry, but the real work of preparing His disciples for the task that would soon be theirs was done in private. He totally associated Himself with the Twelve, making out of them the disciples and disciple-makers they became after His ascension.

CHAPTER 9

ASSOCIATION
WITH JESUS

Robert E. Coleman

". . . Lo, I am with you always. . ." (Matthew 28:20, NKJV)

HE STAYED WITH THEM

Having called His men, Jesus made it a practice to be with them. This was the essence of His training program – just letting His disciples follow Him.

When one stops to think of it, this was an incredibly simple way of doing it. Jesus had no formal school, no seminaries, no outlined course of study, no periodic membership classes in which He enrolled His followers. None of these highly organized procedures considered so necessary today entered at all into His ministry. Amazing as it may seem, all Jesus did to teach these men His way was to draw them close to Himself. He was His own school and curriculum.

The natural informality of this teaching method of Jesus stood in striking contrast to the formal, almost scholastic procedures of the scribes. These religious teachers insisted that their disciples adhere strictly to certain rituals and formulas of knowledge, whereby they were distinguished from others; whereas Jesus asked only that His disciples follow Him. Knowledge was not communicated by the Master in terms of laws and dogmas, but in the living personality of One who walked among them. His disciples were distinguished not by outward conformity to certain rituals, but by being with Him and thereby participating in His doctrine (John 18:19).

TO KNOW WAS TO BE WITH

It was by virtue of this fellowship that the disciples were permitted *"to know the mysteries of the Kingdom of God."* (Luke 8:10, ASV) Knowledge was gained by association before it was understood by explanation. This was not better expressed than when one of the band asked, *"How can we know the way?"* Whereupon Jesus replied, *"I am the way and the truth and the life."* (John 14:6); which was to say that the point in question was already answered, if the disciples would but open their eyes to the spiritual reality incarnated in their midst.

This simple methodology was revealed from the beginning by the invitation that Jesus gave to those He wanted to lead. John and Andrew were invited to *"come and see"* the place where Jesus stayed (John 1:39). Nothing more was said, according to the Record. Yet what more needed to be said? At home with Jesus, they could talk things over and there in private see intimately into His nature and work. Philip was addressed in the same essential manner: *"Follow me."* (John 1:43) Evidently impressed by this simple approach, Philip invited Nathaniel also to *"come and see"* the Master (John 1:46). One living sermon is worth a hundred explanations. Later when James, John, Peter, and Andrew were found mending their nets, Jesus reminded them in the same familiar words, *"Come, follow Me,"* only this time adding the reason for it: *"and I will make you fishers of men."* (Mark 1:17; cf. Matthew 4:19; Luke 5:10) Likewise, Matthew was called from the tax collector's booth with the same invitation, *"Follow me."* (Matthew 9:9; Mark 2:14; Luke 5:27)

THE PRINCIPLE OBSERVED

See the tremendous strategy of it. By responding to this initial call, believers in effect enrolled themselves in the Master's school where their understanding could be enlarged and their faith established. There were certainly many things these men did not understand – things they themselves freely acknowledged as they walked with Him; but all these problems could be dealt with as they followed Jesus. In His presence, they could learn all they needed to know. This principle, which was implied from the start, was given specific articulation later when Jesus chose from the larger group about Him the Twelve *"that they might be with Him."* (Mark 3:14; cf. Luke 6:13) He added, of course, that He was going to send them forth *"to preach, and to have authority to drive out demons."* (Mark 3:15); but often we fail to realize what came first. Jesus made it clear that before these men were *"to preach"* or *"to cast out devils,"* they were to be *"with Him."* In fact, this personal appointment to be in constant association with Him was as much a part of their ordination commission as the authority to evangelize. Indeed, it was for the moment even more important, for it was the necessary preparation for the other.

CLOSER AS TRAINING ENDS

The determination with which Jesus sought to fulfill this commission becomes evident as one reads through the subsequent Gospel accounts. Contrary to what one might expect, as the ministry of Christ lengthened into the second and third years, He gave increasingly more time to the chosen disciples, not less. Some scholars have contended that, prior to the ordination of the apostles, Jesus' first concern was with the multitudes while afterward the emphasis shifted to the disciples, and especially to the Twelve. Whether such a decisive division of concern is justified from the record or not, the fact is clear that Jesus did increasingly give Himself to the apostolic company as time went on.

Frequently, He would take them with Him to some mountainous area of the country where He was relatively unknown, seeking to avoid publicity as far as possible. They took trips together to Tyre and Sidon to the northwest (Matthew 15:21; Mark 7:24), to the *"region of the Decapolis"* (Mark 7:31; cf. Matthew 15:29), *"the region of Dalmanutha"* to the southeast of Galilee (Mark 8:10; cf. Matthew 15:39), and to the *"villages around Caesarea Philippi"* to the northeast (Mark 8:27; cf. Matthew 16:13). These journeys were made partly because of the opposition of the Pharisees and the hostility of Herod, but primarily because Jesus felt the need to be alone with His disciples. Later He spent several months with His disciples in Perea east of the Jordan (Matthew 19:1-20:34; Mark 10:1-52; Luke 13:22-19:27; John 10:40-11:54). As opposition mounted there, *"Jesus no longer moved about publicly among the Jews. Instead, He withdrew to a region near the desert, to a village called Ephraim, where He stayed with His disciples."* (John 11:54) When at last the time came for Him to go to Jerusalem, He significantly *"took the twelve disciples aside"* from the rest as He made His way slowly to the city (Matthew 20:17; cf. Mark 10:32).

In view of this, it is not surprising that during passion week, Jesus scarcely ever let His disciples out of His sight. Even when He prayed alone in Gethsemane, His disciples were only a stone's throw away (Luke 22:41). Is this not the way it is with every family as the hour of departing draws near? Every minute is cherished because of the growing realization that such close association in the flesh soon will be no more. Words uttered under these circumstances are always more precious. Indeed, it was not until their time together began to come to a close that the disciples of Christ were prepared to grasp many of the deeper meanings of His presence with them (John 16:4). Doubtless this explains why the writers of the Gospels were constrained to devote so much of their attention to these last days. Fully half of all that is recorded about Jesus happened in the last months of His life, and most of this in the last week.

The course followed by Jesus through life was supremely portrayed in the days following His resurrection. Interestingly enough, every one of the ten post-resurrection appearances of Christ was to His followers, particularly the chosen apostles.

This fact was impressively recognized by the disciples, as Peter said, *"God raised Him from the dead on the third day and caused Him to be seen. He was not seen by all the people, but by witnesses whom God had already chosen – by us who ate and drank with Him after He rose from the dead."* (Acts 10:40 & 41)

So far as the Bible shows, not a single unbelieving person was permitted to see the glorified Lord. Yet it is not so strange. There was no need to excite the multitudes with His spectacular revelation. What could they have done? But the disciples who had fled in despair following the crucifixion needed to be revived in their faith and confirmed in their mission to the world. His whole ministry evolved around them.

And so it was. The time Jesus invested in these few disciples was so much more by comparison to that given to others that it can only be regarded as a deliberate strategy. He actually spent more time with His disciples than with everybody else in the world put together. He ate with them, slept with them, and talked with them for most of His entire active ministry. They walked together along the lonely roads; they visited together in the crowded cities; they sailed and fished together on the Sea of Galilee; they prayed together in the deserts and in the mountains; and they worshiped together in the synagogues and in the temple.

STILL MINISTERING TO THE MASSES

In addition, we must not overlook that even while Jesus was ministering to others, the disciples were always there with Him. Whether He addressed the multitudes that pressed upon Him, conversed with the scribes and Pharisees who sought to ensnare Him, or spoke to some lonely beggar along the road, the disciples were close at hand to observe and listen. In this way, Jesus' time was paying double dividends. Without neglecting His regular ministry to those in need, He maintained a constant ministry to His disciples by having them with Him. They were thus getting the benefit of everything He said and did to others, plus their own personal explanation and counsel.

IT TAKES TIME

Such close and constant association, of course, meant that Jesus had virtually no time to call His own. Like little children clamoring for the attention of their father, the disciples were always underfoot. Even the time He went apart to keep His personal devotions was subject to interruption at the disciples' need (Mark 6:46-48; cf. Luke 11:1). But Jesus would have it no other way. He wanted to be with them. They were His spiritual children (Mark 10:24; John 13:33), and the only way that a father can properly raise a family is to be with them.

THE FOUNDATION OF FOLLOW-UP

Nothing is more obvious yet more neglected than the application of this principle. By its very nature, it does not call attention to itself, and one is prone to overlook the commonplace. Yet Jesus would not let His disciples miss it. During the last days of His journey, the Master especially felt it necessary to crystallize in their thinking what He had been doing. For example, at one time, turning to those who had followed Him for three years, Jesus said, *"You must also testify, for you have been with Me from the beginning."* (John 15:27) Without any fanfare, and unnoticed by the world, Jesus was saying that He had been training men to be His witnesses after He would leave them, and His method of doing it was simply by being *"with them."* Indeed, as He said on another occasion, it was because they had *"stood by"* Him in His trials that they were appointed to be leaders in His eternal kingdom, where they would each eat and drink at His table and sit on thrones judging the twelve tribes of Israel (Luke 22:28-30).

It would be wrong to assume however that this principle of personal follow-up was confined only to the apostolic band. Jesus concentrated Himself upon these chosen men, but to a lesser and varying degree, He manifested the same concern with others who followed Him. For example, He went home with Zaccheus after his conversion on the street of Jericho (Luke 19:7), and He spent some time with him before leaving the city. After the conversion of the woman at the weil in Samaria, Jesus stayed two extra days in Sychar to instruct the people of that community who *"believed in Him because of the woman's testimony."* Because of that personal association with them, *"many more became believers,"* not because of the woman's witness, but because they heard the Master for themselves (John 4:39-42). Often one who received some help from the Master would be permitted to join the procession following Jesus, as for example, Bartimaeus (Matthew 20:34; Mark 10:52; Luke 18:43). In such a way, many attached themselves to the apostolic company as is evidenced by the seventy with Him in the later Judean ministry (Luke 10:1 & 17). All of these believers received some personal attention, but it could not be compared to that given to the Twelve.

Mention should be made, too, of that group of faithful women who helped support Jesus and the disciples out of their own means, such as Mary and Martha (Luke 10:38-42), Mary Magdalene, Joanna, Susanna, *"and many others"* (Luke 8:1-3). Some of these women were with Him to the end. He certainly did not refuse their gracious kindness and often took the occasion to help them in their faith. Nevertheless, Jesus was well aware of the sex barrier, and although He welcomed their assistance, did not try to incorporate these women into the select company of His chosen disciples. In this kind of follow-up there are limitations that one must recognize.

But apart from the rules of propriety, Jesus did not have the time to personally give all these people, men or women, constant attention. He did all that He could, and this doubtless served to impress upon His disciples the need for immediate personal care of new converts, but He had to devote Himself primarily to the task of developing some men who, in turn, could give this kind of personal attention to others.

THE CHURCH AS A CONTINUING FELLOWSHIP

Really the whole problem of giving personal care to every believer is resolved only in a thorough understanding of the nature and mission of the church. It is well to observe here that the emergence of the church principle around Jesus, whereby one believer was brought into fellowship with all others, was the practice in a larger dimension of the same thing that He was doing with the Twelve.

One cannot help but observe in this connection that the references to "the disciples" as a corporate body are much more frequent in the Gospels than are references to an individual disciple. When it is remembered that these accounts were written under inspiration by the disciples, and not Jesus, it is quite significant that they would set forth their own place in such terms. We need not infer from this that the disciples were unimportant as individuals, for such was not the case, but it does impress on us the fact that the disciples understood that their Lord looked upon them as a body of believers being trained together for a common mission. Through Christ, they saw themselves first as a church, and secondly as individuals within that body.

Actually, it was the church that was the means of following up all those who followed Him. That is, the group of believers became the body of Christ, and as such, ministered to each other individually and collectively.

Every member of the community of faith had a part to fulfill in this ministry. But this they could do only as they themselves were trained and inspired. As long as Jesus was with them in the flesh, He was the Leader, but afterward, it was necessary for those in the church to assume this leadership. Again, this meant that Jesus had to train them to do it, and this involved His own constant personal association with a few chosen men.

OUR PROBLEM

When will the church learn this lesson? Preaching to the masses, although necessary, will never suffice in the work of preparing leaders for evangelism. Nor can occasional prayer meetings and training classes for Christian workers do this job. Building disciples is not that easy. It requires constant personal attention, much like that which a father gives to his children. This is something that no organization or class can ever do. Children are not raised by proxy. The example of Jesus teaches us that it can only be done by persons staying right with those they seek to lead.

The church obviously has failed at this point, and failed tragically. There is a lot of talk in the church about evangelism and Christian nurture, but little concern for personal association when it becomes evident that such work involves the sacrifice of personal indulgence. Of course, most churches insist on bringing new members through some kind of a new believer class that usually meets an hour a week for a month or so. But the rest of the time, the young convert has no contact at all with a definite Christian training program, except in worship services and Sunday school. Unless the new Christian, if indeed he is saved, has parents or friends who will fill the gap in a real way, he is left on his own to find the solutions to innumerable practical problems, any one of which could mean disaster to his faith.

With such haphazard follow-up of believers, it is no wonder that about half of those who make professions and join the church eventually fall away or lose the glow of a Christian experience, and that fewer still grow in sufficient knowledge and grace to be of any real service to the kingdom. If Sunday services and membership training classes are all that a church has for developing young converts into mature disciples, then they are defeating their own purpose by contributing to a false security. There is simply no substitute for getting with people, and it is ridiculous to imagine that anything less, short of a miracle, can develop strong Christian leadership. After all, if Jesus, the Son of God, found it necessary to stay almost constantly with His few disciples for three years, how can a church expect to do this job on an assembly line basis a few days out of the year?

THE PRINCIPLE APPLIED TODAY

Clearly, the policy of Jesus at this point teaches us that whatever method of follow-up the church adopts, it must have as its basis a personal guardian concern for those entrusted to its care. To do otherwise is essentially to abandon new believers to the devil.

This means that some system must be found by which every convert is given a Christian friend to follow until such time as he or she can lead another. This friend should stay with the new believer as much as possible, studying the Bible and praying together, all the while answering questions, clarifying the truth, and seeking to help others together. If a church does not have such committed members willing to do this service, then it should be training some.

THE NEED FOR MULTIPLYING DISCIPLES

LeRoy Eims

LeRoy Eims, Director of Public Ministry for The Navigators, has been practicing what he writes about for more than forty years.

Eims is a popular and effective speaker at conferences and has ministered in churches, seminaries, and Bible schools throughout the world. He is the author of books on Christian leadership, Christian living, and discipleship. This chapter is excerpted from his first chapter in *The Lost Art of Disciple Making* (Grand Rapids: Zondervan, 1978).

One of Eim's gifts is being able to illustrate Biblical truths and concepts with vivid, down-to-earth, contemporary illustrations. We used to call these "war stories," and Eims – with his experience in the United States Marine Corps in World War II and many years of productive ministry to servicemen with the Navigators – has a myriad of them. This chapter contains some classic stories of how disciple-making really works in our time; what happened in the lives of Joe, Johnny, Roy, and LeRoy himself are unforgettable and challenging to all of us. So let us be challenged and commit ourselves to having this kind of methodology in our own ministry.

THE NEED FOR MULTIPLYING DISCIPLES

LeRoy Eims

"And the word of God increased; and the number of the disciples multiplied in Jerusalem greatly." (Acts 6:7, KJV)

One day, I received a phone call from a busy pastor. "Could we get together," he asked, "Someplace, sometime to talk about training people in my church?" He was willing to fly anywhere in the United States to meet me and discuss his problem for half a day or so. He obviously needed help, so we set up a meeting.

As we spent some time together, I found his situation to be fairly typical. He was the pastor of a growing, healthy, and flourishing church. People were coming to Christ, attendance had increased, and he had to have two morning worship services. God was clearly blessing his church in many wonderful ways.

But this pastor also had a problem. He knew that unless he trained some spiritually qualified workers among the men and women of his congregation, people would not get needed help in the initial stages of Christian growth (adequate follow-up) and would not develop into strong, robust disciples of Jesus Christ. And the pastor knew he was the key to this. The whole process had to begin with him. He could not toss it to a "department," nor delegate it to someone else. As the spiritual leader of these people, he had to lead the way.

He had another problem – he was already a busy man. Many things demanded his attention; many people demanded his time. Like many other pastors, he spent a good deal of his time putting

175

out brush fires in his congregation. No sooner had he dealt with one problem than another one arose.

To his consternation and frustration, he spent too much time with problem-centered people, trying to settle quarrels, make peace between members, deal with difficult family situations, and a hundred and one other things.

But he had a dream. At times, he would go into his study, lock the door, and think of his situation in a whole new light. *Wouldn't it be great,* he would think to himself, *if I had a dedicated, ever-growing band of spiritually qualified men and women who could help handle some of the spiritual problems that keep coming up in this church?* He meant a band of people who knew how to win another person to Christ and then take that person from the time of his conversion and help him become a solid, dedicated, committed, fruitful, mature disciple who could in time repeat that process in the life of another.

He would smile there in the privacy of his study, for his dream was so vivid he could almost reach out and touch what he envisioned. But then he would be jarred back to reality by the ringing of the phone. Another problem. And he was the only spiritually qualified person in the congregation who could help. So he would set aside his dream, pick up his Bible, and go out the door.

DISCIPLES IN ACTION

Let's look at another scene. Four couples are meeting for a Bible study on a weeknight. They have been getting together for about four months, ever since three of them had been converted to Christ. One of the laymen in the church has been leading the study, and they have just settled down for one of their lively discussions. As they launch into their lesson, the phone rings.

"Is Joe there?" Joe is one of the four-month-old Christians.

"Yes, but he's busy right now. He's in a Bible study."

The voice is desperate. "Please! I've got to talk with him."

"OK."

Joe picks up the phone and listens. "OK," he says, "I'll come right over."

Joe comes back to his Bible study group and explains. His business partner wants him to come over and help him. There's been a marital fight, and the man's wife is walking out on him. The whole mess has been brewing for a long time, and Joe feels he should go and do what he can.

The leader of the study group says he thinks it's the right thing to do, and while Joe's gone, the group will pray. So Joe, a four-month-old Christian, picks up his Bible and goes out the door to try to save a marriage. The Bible study turns into a prayer meeting.

That scene is a real situation with real people. The leader of that group told me about it a few days after it happened. At the time, he hadn't heard from Joe on how his meeting with his partner had gone. I saw that leader again about three weeks later and heard the great news. Joe had been used by God to lead both husband and wife to Christ. He was now in the process of leading them in a study of the Scriptures.

The leader, in turn, began to spend a little extra time with Joe to answer some of his questions now that he and his wife were leading new Christians in a study of the Word of God. Though Joe had always been eager to study the Bible, he was more so now. He needed a great deal of help and knew it. The leader was only too glad to do what he could. He could see that the Lord was using that time to deepen their relationship and to deepen Joe's life in the Lord.

It was also a challenge to the other couples in Joe's study group. It had become evident to them that sooner or later the Lord would give them an opportunity to share with others some of the things they were learning. It made the study that much more meaningful to all of them.

That scene, with variations, is being repeated in many places around the world. It is not an isolated incident. In fact, the story of the pastor who met with me, mentioned earlier in this chapter, has a happy ending. After we'd spent the day together discussing follow-up and training workers, he went back to his church and began putting into practice the principles I shared with him and that are taught in this chapter. Today, there is a steady stream of disciples and workers who emerge from his ministry to affect their neighborhoods and friends for Christ. These people from his church are being used by God to win others to Christ and to help their converts, in turn, repeat the process.

This concept of multiplying disciples has not always been so widely accepted as it is today. At one time, in fact not too long ago, relatively few people were doing it. But many more today are returning to that Biblical process.

THE CRUCIAL ELEMENT OF PERSONAL HELP

Shortly after my wife, Virginia, and I became Christians, we met Waldron Scott, a young man about our age who took a personal interest in us. He had been helped in his Christian life by a fellow serviceman while stationed on Guam with the Air Force in World War II. We were classmates in college, and he came over to our home once a week or so to share spiritual truths with us and to help us in our growth.

His actual working with us began on the day I asked him why there seemed to be such an obvious difference in our Christian lives, why he was like he was and Virginia and I were like we were. He was able to quote the Scriptures; fairly regularly he would tell how God had answered his prayers; he seemed to know his Bible well.

He came over that night and asked me some questions. Did I read my Bible regularly? No, hardly ever. Did I study it? Again, no. Did I memorize it? Aha, here I had him. The previous Sunday our pastor had preached on Matthew 6:33, and I had been so impressed by the verse that I memorized it when I got home.

"Great," Scotty said. "Quote it for me. Let's hear it."

I couldn't remember it. I realized then that there was something lacking in my Scripture memory program.

Then he asked, "Do you pray?"

"Well, yes," I told him. "At mealtimes I repeat a prayer I have memorized." We were just sitting down for some refreshments, so I said my prayer: "Bless the food which now we take to do us good for Jesus' sake. Amen."

During the course of the evening it became obvious that there was much more to prayer than that. He offered to meet with my wife and me and share some of the things that had been of help to him. We were eager to do so.

We began. Scotty taught us how to read the Bible and get something out of our reading. He taught us how to do personal Bible study and, with the help of the Holy Spirit, apply its lessons to our lives. He taught us to memorize the Word so that it would be available to the Holy Spirit twenty-four hours a day. He taught us how to assimilate the Scriptures into the spiritual bloodstream of our lives through meditation on the Word. He taught us how to pray and expect answers from God. That was a blessed year for us. We were eager to learn, and Scotty was willing to spend time with us.

The next year I began my sophomore year, and Scotty continued to meet with us. We were continuing to grow and my Christian life was full of new discoveries. We had discovered the high adventure of abundant Christian living as the Lord was becoming more personal and real in our lives.

Midway through the first semester, a classmate came up to me and said, "You know, LeRoy, I've been watching you. Your Christian life is sure on a different plane than mine." And he began asking some questions, essentially what I had asked Scotty the year before.

I smiled. "Well, do you read your Bible regularly?"

"No."

"Do you study it?" No again.

"Do you memorize the Scriptures?" No, he didn't do that either.

"Do you pray?" Still no.

I suggested we get together and talk about these things. He was eager and enthusiastic, so we began. I shared with him the things Scotty had shared with me, and he began to grow in his Christian life. He began to dig into the Word, pray, and witness, and the Spirit of God worked mightily in his life that year.

The following year I transferred to the University of Washington, and my friend transferred to another school. A few months after school began, I received an interesting letter from him. He had been attending a Christian fellowship on campus, and a fellow student had come up to him and asked him about his Christian life. It seemed this student had noticed a difference and wanted to find out about it. So my friend asked him some questions that had to do with Bible reading, study, memory, and prayer. He had shown a keen interest in doing these things, so my friend had begun to share with him on a regular basis the things he had learned from me and that I had learned from Scotty.

Meanwhile, a Christian student had come up to me on the University of Washington campus . . . and so it goes. For many years now, I have been involved in helping others personally in their Christian lives. I've watched the interest that pastors, missionaries, dedicated laymen, college and seminary students, and servicemen have shown in helping others individually as well. Today, a growing groundswell of interest in multiplying disciples is to be seen in many churches and by many people.

TO MULTIPLY OR NOT TO MULTIPLY – THAT IS THE QUESTION

Some years ago, I was talking to a zealous young Christian. "Bob," I asked, "What's the thing that brings you more joy than anything else in life?"

"Man, LeRoy, that's easy," he replied. "Leading someone to Christ."

I agreed with him. "Everybody is happy when that happens – you are happy, the new convert is happy, and there is joy in heaven. But there is something even greater than that."

He was puzzled. What could possibly be greater than seeing a person come to Christ?

I continued, "When the person you have led to Christ grows and develops into a dedicated, fruitful, mature disciple who then goes on to lead others to Christ and help them in turn as well."

"Say!" he exclaimed, "I've never thought of that!"

Frankly, it is no surprise that he hadn't heard or thought of that. In those days the idea was pretty obscure, but he was willing to take the time to learn, and he did. Today there are many mature, committed, fruitful disciples on two continents because of the impact of Bob's life and his vision of multiplying disciples.

On the other hand, a lack of knowledge of these things can have sad consequences. I was visiting a foreign mission field and spoke with a veteran missionary. He told me a story that still haunts me; I can't get it out of my mind. He had gone overseas some fifteen years before we met and began the usual programs. About the time he arrived on his field, he met a young man named Johnny who was involved in something quite different.

Johnny was a committed disciple of Jesus Christ, but he was going about his ministry in all the wrong ways according to the "book." In contrast to the typical missionary approach of the time, Johnny was spending the bulk of his time meeting with a few young men in that country. The veteran missionary tried to get Johnny straightened out, but the young man kept on with his "different" approach. The years passed, and the veteran missionary now had to leave the country of his service due to new visa restrictions. As he sat across the coffee table from me in his home, he told me, "LeRoy, I've got little to show for my time there. Oh, there is a group of people who meet in our assembly, but I wonder what will happen to them when I leave. They are not disciples. They have been faithful in listening to my sermons, but they do not witness. Few of them know how to lead another person to Christ. They know nothing about discipling others. And now that I am leaving, I can see I've all but wasted my time here."

He continued, "Then I look at what has come out of Johnny's life. One of the men he worked with is now a professor at the university. This man is mightily used of God to reach and train scores of university students. Another is leading a witnessing and discipling team of about forty young men and women. Another is in a nearby city with a group of thirty-five growing disciples around him. Three have gone to other countries as missionaries and are now leading teams who are multiplying disciples. God is blessing their work."

"I see the contrast between my life and his, and it is tragic. I was so sure I was right. What he was doing seemed so insignificant, but now I look at the results and they are staggering." It was a sad meeting for both of us.

On another occasion, I was speaking at a weekend conference in the Midwest. A pastor who had spent the bulk of his life as a missionary in the Middle East and was now in a nearby city came to the conference. In the opening meeting, I shared this passage with the conferees: *"It was He who gave some to be apostles, some to be prophets, some to be evangelists, and some to be pastors and teachers, to prepare God's people for works of service, so that the body of Christ may be built up."* (Ephesians 4:11 & 12)

I tried to explain that the thrust of that passage was that God had given leaders to the church in order to build up and train the rest of us in the work of the ministry. I said that the ministry of the Gospel was to be done by all of us – laymen and clergy alike. All of us together are to be a great witnessing brotherhood, but we need training.

After the meeting, this man came up to me and held out his Greek New Testament. "That's exactly what it says," he stated.

With that he turned and walked away, went to his room, packed his bags, and started to leave the conference. I was startled by his actions, so I stopped him and asked if we had offended him in some way. Was there anything for which we should apologize and ask his forgiveness?

"Not at all," he replied. "I've got all I need. My people are going to hear about this!" With that he got into his car and drove off. He simply wanted to be back with his people that very Sunday, preach to them that very message, and begin practicing it in his ministry.

In recent years, I have watched the country where he had served for so many years blow up with bitter hatred and racial strife. I've often wondered if it might have been a different story had he gone there thirty years ago with the vision of discipling a band of men and women, something like Johnny had done on another mission field.

One spring, a colleague of mine and I taught a workshop at a seminary in their School of Evangelism. The workshop ran for three days and was well attended. Our topic was "Discipleship in the Local Church."

During one of our discussion sessions, an elderly pastor spoke up and told us of his own experience in discipling some of the men in his church. He had started this about three years before and now had a band of stalwart, faithful men on whom he could call at a moment's notice. He had started with one man; later he and this man worked with two others who had expressed interest. The discipling process continued, and after a time the four of them began to meet with four others. The ministry had multiplied till he now had this dedicated band of men who were truly spiritually qualified to work in the ministry of the church.

The elderly pastor told us it was by far the most rewarding, fulfilling, and exciting thing that had happened to him in thirty-five years in the ministry. After this account, the eyes of many of the young seminarians began to gleam with anticipation. They could hardly wait to get out into the pastorate and begin their own ministry of multiplying disciples.

THE INDIANAPOLIS MODEL

Dr. Roy Blackwood has been a close personal friend of mine for years. He has been multiplying disciples since he went to Indianapolis, Indiana, to form a new congregation in his denomination.

He determined to build his ministry on the philosophy of spiritual multiplication.

He did not want to be just a Bible teacher to a group of spiritually hungry souls who would get their only ration of spiritual food once a week from his sermons. He wanted to train a band of strong, rugged soldiers of the Cross who would then collaborate with him in the work of the ministry in the church.

Some years have now passed, and his ministry has proved to be one of the unique expressions of discipleship in our day. Roy has his disciples. In fact, when he and his wife went around the world on a preaching and lecture tour, he left the church in the able hands of the people whom he had trained and was gone for almost a year.

During his absence, the men preached the sermons and directed the activities of the church. They *did* the ministry, and the Lord blessed their efforts as the congregation grew and flourished under their leadership.

Some years ago, a man came to me with what he thought was a great idea. He was bubbling over with enthusiasm and was eager to secure my participation in his plan to forward the work of Christ. So I listened carefully. When he had finished, I declined his offer to become involved. He was surprised and asked why I would not work with him.

"Two reasons," I replied. "One it is not Scriptural. Two, it won't work."

What I enjoy so much about this approach to ministry is that it is Scriptural and it works. In the first place, it is a Scriptural approach to helping fulfill Christ's Great Commission (Matthew 28:18-20) and helping to do something about training workers (Matthew 9:37 & 38), who today, as in Christ's day, are still few.

Second, I have seen it in action for over thirty-five years and it works. When some of us were involved in a ministry of multiplying disciples in the 1950s, we didn't have it well codified and organized. We just called it "working with a few men (or women)." But since those days, I've watched pastors, homemakers, missionaries, nurses, building contractors, school teachers, seminary professors, and grocery-store owners get involved in the lives of a few people. I have seen the Lord bless their efforts and multiply their lives in Christ into the lives of others.

This is not a cure-all of course, but few things are. But I do know this. When you start spending individual time with another

Christian for the purpose of having a ministry in his or her life –
time together in the Word, prayer, fellowship, systematic training –
something happens in your own life as well. May God grant you
patience, love, and perseverance as you begin to share with others
the life He has given you.

CHAPTER 11

DISCIPLESHIP AS A LIFESTYLE

Gene Warr

One of the most experienced and dedicated disciple-makers we will find anywhere in the world today is Gene Warr, a layman and businessman in Oklahoma City. He is the President of the Warr Company, a real-estate investment corporation, and the author of *The Godly Man*, a practical Bible study for men. This chapter is taken from his book *Making Disciples* (Fort Worth, Texas: International Evangelism Association, 1986), which is essential to the library of every disciple-maker.

Lorne Sanny, President of The Navigators, wrote these significant words in the foreward: "Gene Warr is a disciple-maker. He is also a stimulator. He has been doing it for years and getting others to do it. Therefore, the material presented in this book has been tested in real-life experience. It is a veritable handbook of how-to's for those who are willing to obey Jesus' command to *'go and make disciples.'*" It couldn't be stated any better than that.

This chapter deals with some necessary negatives, warnings of the cost of ministry, and certain misconceptions some people have about the disciple-making approach. But Warr's inimitable style will make us willing to pay the cost and help us overcome any misconceptions we might have had.

CHAPTER 11

DISCIPLESHIP AS A LIFESTYLE

Gene Warr

"And the things that thou hast heard of me among many witnesses, the same commit thou to faithful men, who shall be able to teach others also." (2 Timothy 2:2, KJV)

Multiplication works. It is God's time-tested plan for ministry. Disciples have been made over the centuries, and now there are representatives of Christianity in every nation on earth. Moses poured his life into Joshua; Elijah poured his life into Elisha; and on and on. Jesus to the Twelve; the Twelve to others; Paul to Timothy; Timothy to faithful men; those faithful men to others also.

WHY I AM COMMITTED TO A MULTIPLICATION MINISTRY

I am committed to a multiplication ministry for three reasons: the brevity of life, a sense of stewardship, and a desire for my life to count for God.

First, *the brevity of life.* The Bible teaches that life is like a vapor. Swifter than a weaver's shuttle, it is like a tale that is told. It is fleeting, like water that is poured out upon the ground and cannot be gathered up again. I can identify with David when he cried out, *"Cast me not off in the time of old age; forsake me not when my strength faileth."* (Psalm 71:9, KJV) I understand that. And

187

when David prayed, *"Now also when I am old and gray-headed, O God, forsake me not; until I have showed Thy strength unto this generation, and Thy power to every one that is to come."* (Psalm 71:18 KJV)

The only way I can show the power of God to *"everyone who is to come"* is by investing in the lives of people who will invest in the lives of other people who will invest . . . and that way, by the grace of God, I can show the power of God to generations yet to come.

There are even some promises regarding this: *"Even to old age I am the same and to (the time of) gray hair I will bear you. I have made you and I will carry you: even I will bear you and save you."* (Isaiah 46:4, LB) A psalm promises, *"In old age they shall still be bearing fruit. They shall be full of life and vitality."* (Psalm 92:14, LB)

Second, *a sense of stewardship.* We refer to life as "my life." It is precious. In Job 2:4 Satan says, *"All that a man hath will he give for his life."* (KJV) But why do we call it *"my* life?" I have a responsibility for the life that God has given me. I didn't manufacture it. I don't sustain it. It is something God has loaned me for a short time while I am here on earth, and I believe I have a responsibility to invest it where it will count most. The psalmist says, *"Let everyone bless God and sing His praises, for He holds our lives in His hands. And He holds our feet to the path."* (Psalm 66:8-9 LB)

Third, *I want my life to count for something worthwhile.* I'd hate to reach the end of the road and have it said of me as it was said of an old couple in Somerset Maugham's *Of Human Bondage:* "It was as if they had never lived at all." I don't want that to happen to me. I want to *live* and pass on abundant life in Christ to many, many others. I can do it through a ministry of spiritual multiplication, reproducing myself many times over in a disciple-making ministry. And so can you.

DISCIPLE-MAKING IS A COSTLY MINISTRY

To be used of God to make disciples, we must be willing to pay the price . . . and it is a costly ministry.

Costly in Quantity of Time. We must be constantly on call. It takes time to drive to a restaurant to eat a meal with the person we are training. It takes time to go on a trip with that trainee. And it takes time to do other things that will make a reproducing disciple of him. Moses prayed, *"So teach us to number our days, that we may apply our hearts unto wisdom."* (Psalm 90:12, KJV) Our time will not be our own. We must be available to those whom God has called us to help.

Costly in Lack of Recognition. Paul said, *"Yet we urge you to have more and more of this love, and to make it your ambition to have no ambition! Be busy with your own affairs and do your work yourselves. The result will be a reputation for honesty in the world outside and an honorable independence."* (1 Thessalonians 4:11-12 Phillips) The ministry of follow-up and assimilation is not the kind that gets wide publicity in the church paper. Neither is there a place to check it on our offering envelopes. Discipling has traditionally been an unrecognized work in the kingdom of God.

Costly in Inconvenience. We are servants of those we intend to help. Jesus said, *"I am among you as one who serves."* (Luke 22:27) We must meet the needs of those God has chosen for us to help. And this means leaving the television during a Dallas – Los Angeles playoff game, with the score tied and only a few minutes to play, when a call for help has come from the person I am training. We meet these needs on God's terms, not ours. We are servants to the body of Christ.

Costly in Hurt. At times we will be hurt by those we are trying to help. On this subject Paul wrote, *"And I will very gladly spend and be spent for you; though the more abundantly I love you, the less I be loved."* (2 Corinthians 12:15, KJV) In the same letter he added, *"I pray that you will live good lives, not because that will be a feather in our caps, proving that what we teach is right; no, for we want you to do right even if we ourselves are despised."* (2 Corinthians 13:7, LB) Paul was willing to suffer the cost of being despised if the hurt would help the Corinthians. He went on, *"We are glad to be weak and despised if you are really strong. Our greatest wish and prayer is that you will become mature Christians."* (2 Corinthians 13:9, LB) Some in whom you have invested your life will turn their backs on you and walk away. Others may even become bitter toward you. Still others will go only so far in the school of discipleship and no further. All of these will hurt you. You must not become discouraged in your calling, for some of those who fall by the wayside will eventually come back and want to get back on the path. Others are certainly better off for the help they have received than if they had received none at all.

Costly in Vulnerability to Exposure. Paul wrote to Timothy: *"But thou hast fully known my doctrine, manner of life, purpose, faith, longsuffering, charity, patience, persecutions, afflictions, which came unto me at Antioch, at Iconium, at Lystra; what persecutions I endured: but out of them all the Lord delivered me."* (2 Timothy 3:10 & 11, KJV) In the Phillips translation, this same verse reads: *"But you, Timothy, have known intimately both what I have taught and how I have lived. My purpose and my faith are not secrets to you. You saw my endurance and love and patience as I met all those persecutions and difficulties."*

You can't hide from the one you are helping. The one you are helping will see your feet of clay. A disciple will know your weaknesses because on an eyeball-to-eyeball basis, there is no place to hide.

Costly in Seeing Your Weaknesses Reproduced. As it is in nature, so it is true in the Spirit: we produce in kind.

This is why "cross training" is so important. This happens naturally in the church through the numerous relationships made in Sunday school and in the worship services. In cross training, the disciple gets spiritual help from others besides you, so that not all of your weaknesses are reproduced in that one. What Samuel learned as a little boy in Eli's family (bad habits of child-rearing), he reproduced in his own children. Then, at the end of Samuel's life, the people saw the grave weaknesses in his children and asked that his children not be the rulers over them. A king had to be chosen from elsewhere. We do reproduce in kind.

Costly in Your Life. This is the main price we pay if we are going to disciple people. God said through Isaiah to his people Israel: *"Since thou wast precious in My sight, thou hast been honorable, and I have loved thee: therefore will I give men for thee, and people for thy life."* (43:4 KJV) That is exactly what it will cost you – your life.

MISCONCEPTIONS ABOUT THE MINISTRY OF DISCIPLE-MAKING

Because the ministry of multiplication is so effective, it will be fought tooth and nail by our enemy the devil. He will strive to combat it in every way possible, and one of his best tools is to use misconceptions. We need to be alert to these to fulfill our ministries of disciple-making. There are a number of misconceptions that can hinder our work:

That an emphasis on discipleship neglects evangelism. Our ministries are not either/or, but both/and. We are not only to follow-up others, but also to win people to Christ. The end result of all one-to-one training develops a lifestyle of spiritual reproduction.

That you have to be a finished product to help others become disciples. You only have to be one step ahead of others to help them down the entire length of the road of life. Even Paul did not claim to be completely mature when he trained Timothy and others.

That you must be an ordained minister to do it. Sometimes even clergymen and theologians do not know how to reach others face-to-face. W. A. Criswell tells the story of a group of modernistic theologians who met with the Lord Jesus. The Lord asked these famous and illustrious theologians, "Who do men say that I am?" And they replied, "Some say that you are John the Baptist raised from the dead; some say that you are Jeremiah or one of the prophets; and even some say you are the Christ, the Son of God." Then the Lord asked the theologians, "But who do you say that I am?" And the theologians gave a learned answer, "Thou art the ground of being, thou art the leap of faith into the impenetrable unknown, thou art the existential, unphraseable, unverbalized, unpropositional confrontation with the infinitude of inherent subjective experience." The Lord turned sadly away.

That it is an unrealistic approach. There is the story of the man who told Dwight L. Moody, the famous evangelist, that he didn't like his method of evangelism. Moody said he wasn't too happy with it himself, then asked the man what method he used. The man answered, "Oh I don't have any method." Moody replied, "Well, I like mine better than yours."

True, if those who had begun the multiplication process thirty-two years ago had succeeded with every convert and disciple, the entire world would by now have been totally reached for Christ. Weak links in the chain break the reproductive process. Every time you lose a link you cut your ultimate production in half. This is the reason why quality discipling is so important.

That you must see immediate, measurable results. It took Jesus three years to train twelve people . . . and really only three men in great depth. Why are *we* in such a hurry? In our society of "instantness" we want instant disciples. There is no such thing in all the history of the church.

That it will always succeed. Obviously, it won't. There will always be weak links. The story of Gehazi, a disciple of Elisha in 2 Kings (5:15 & 16, 21-27), is a good example of this. Gehazi had every opportunity to learn. He saw Elisha heal the city's waters which had produced barrenness; he saw bears attack the young men who had made fun of Elisha; he heard Elisha pray and saw God's answer as He filled ditches with water so that the men and animals could drink when fighting the Moabites; he saw the widow supplied supernaturally with enough oil to sell and pay off her debts and have sufficient remaining to live on; he saw the raising of the dead son of the Shunammite woman; he saw the poisoned pot of vegetables which the sons of the prophets had tasted made pure by Elisha's throwing in a handful of meal; he saw Naaman the leper healed. And yet, in the end, Gehazi failed. One of the great misconceptions in working with people is that you always succeed. You don't.

My own stumbling efforts to make disciples certainly have not always been crowned with success. That's one of the things that breaks my heart. There are many reasons for lack of success:

Compromise for social approval. I remember a young man whom I will call Bill. After some seminary training, Bill came to our city deeply disillusioned with Christianity and his own walk and life. As I began to meet, talk, and pray with him, I found that he knew nothing of the basic disciplines of the Christian life. I shared these with him, and he responded positively to the idea. He began to meet the Lord morning by morning in a quiet time, began to memorize Scripture, was effectively reaching out in witness to others, and was doing an excellent job of in-depth Bible study. He was capable of making a good living with his hands, which he was doing, when one day a small church in Oklahoma City called him to be their pastor. He accepted. The Lord blessed his ministry there and we continued to fellowship. It wasn't long until a larger church in a distant state gave him a call, and he responded. In the larger situation, he was in a more affluent society. He began to drink socially, then steadily began to seek out the companionship of other women, and consequently lost his wife and family. He took his own life in a motel room. My heart yet yearns for him.

Love of money. Then there was another whom I'll call George. George was a sharp fraternity man, socially very acceptable, a good businessman, and was seemingly sitting on top of the world. When he was about thirty years of age, the claims of Christ were made clear to him for the first time and he made that commitment. Then the roof fell in. He lost his job, moved to another city with his family, had difficulty finding employment, but finally, by the grace of God, was able to get a good job. He began to move up in the economic scale again. He continued to walk with the Lord and encourage others, but his desire for wealth began to shade his judgment, and he took a job that put him in compromising positions. Finally, the temptation was too great and he succumbed. He left his wife and children. The last I heard about him was that he had married a widow older than himself and was living on her money. George and I had spent hours together studying the Bible, praying together, and going out on ministry assignments together. Often on my knees weeping in prayer, I wondered and asked God where I had failed him.

Lack of wholeheartedness. Let me tell you about a man whom I'll call Stan. Everyone liked Stan. He had a dear wife. They were active in their church, Sunday school, and home Bible study. For perhaps two years, they were about as faithful a couple as you could see. They grew and grew to a certain point, and then stopped – stagnated.

Today, Stan is relatively ineffective as a husband, as a father, and as a witnessing Christian. There were some issues in his life that he refused to deal with. One was a failure to submit to authority. He held on to a streak of rebelliousness. Another was unfaithfulness – making promises and not keeping them, starting jobs and not completing them. A third issue was his refusal to operate with a margin. This was true with time as well as with money. Fourth, a lack of wholeheartedness. He did things as he wanted to do them instead of making an all-out effort to do them as to the Lord. Fifth, just plain laziness, which in the final analysis is self-centeredness. Today, as I look at Stan and recognize the infinite potential in his life, it grieves me to see him on the shelf outside the will of God.

Conclusion. Stories of failure are sobering. You ask me why I don't quit. The reason I don't is that, thank God, there are other stories, too. They center around a question I am often asked, "Is it really worth investing your life in people?" Let me tell you how worthwhile it is.

Paul was newly married and a youth director in his church. But he was fired from that job – the job he was depending on to support his wife and to see him through school. He was fired, not for doing a poor job as a youth director, but because he couldn't preach – which he had not been hired to do.

I thought the young man should know why he was fired, so I asked him to come down to my office. I told him he was fired because he didn't know how to get along with adults. He had been called to work with young people and had done an excellent job with them, but unless he learned how to get along with adults, he would always be in trouble. I then asked him what he was going to do with his schooling, and at that point he didn't know.

I counseled with Paul for a while, then told him I would help him financially with his schooling, but there would be one requirement on his part. Every time he came to get his monthly check, he would have to spend two hours with me. We started on that basis, and I began to invest my life in his.

Some months later, Paul met a fellow student by the name of Bob and began to invest in his life some of the things I had been sharing with him. Still later, Bob became the youth director in my church, so I carried on with him where Paul had left off. Bob led a pair of twins, Rick and Bob, to Christ, then began to invest his life in theirs. One of them is now a pastor, the other a Christian education director. The first Bob also led Lynn to the Lord, trained him individually over a period of time, and he is now about to enter a Christian-education ministry.

These men have in turn led others to Christ and poured their lives into them, and that chain in the ministry goes on reproducing. And it is only one of a series of chains that began even before Charlie Riggs started investing his life in mine. For Charlie had been trained by Dawson Trotman.

Is it really worth investing our lives in people? As far as I am concerned, it certainly is. Here are seven generations, and the chain is still growing.

    Dawson Trotman
    Charlie Riggs
    Me
    Paul
    Bob
    Rick, Bob, and Lynn
    Many others . . .

Multiplication works. Discipleship as a lifestyle can and will re-produce to many generations.

APPENDIX A
ILLUSTRATIONS AND
AMPLIFICATIONS FOR
ALL SESSIONS

A

SESSION ONE

#1 Amplification: Get Acquainted

From your first meeting together, your Timothy needs to realize that you want to establish a genuine friendship. He needs to know that you are *sincerely concerned about him.* To begin this friendship, you will both need to share different aspects of your lives. He needs to see that you are a well-balanced person who is willing to talk with him about subjects beyond his spiritual needs.

    Concentrate on being a good listener during your meetings. Something is wrong if you find yourself doing all of the talking. Try to establish *good eye contact,* so he will know that your attention is centered on his needs. Pay special attention to areas of his life which need additional prayer or assistance.

#2 Amplification: Determine His Relationship With Christ

Your first objective will be to determine whether or not your Timothy has received Christ as his Lord and Savior. To help do this, lead him through Session One. It is a short Bible study about understanding the Gospel. During this study, you will briefly review *why* we are separated from God, *why* Jesus Christ had to die for our sins, and *what* decision every person must make regarding Christ.

#3 Illustration: The "Pen" and/or the "Cup Of Water"

Seek to show your Timothy the difference between *believing* and *receiving* by using one or both of the following illustrations:

197

a. Pen Illustration:

Hold your pen or pencil and ask your Timothy, "Do you *believe* that I have a pen in my hand?"
"Yes, I do."
"Do you believe it enough, to reach out and take it if I offer it to you?" (Offer it, so he can take it.)
Now ask, "What did you just do?"
"I took it."
"In other words, you *believed* me when I said I would give it to you, and you were willing to *receive* it in simple faith."
He listens,
"The pen was *potentially* yours the moment I decided to give it to you, but it wasn't *experientially* yours until you acted in faith and *received* it."
"What Jesus Christ did for us on the cross was *potentially* for everyone in the world. The *gift* of salvation has already been paid for, and the loving hand of God is now offering that gift to you. He is patiently waiting for every person to admit their need, *believe* in Him, and *receive* His gift of forgiveness and eternal life!"

b. Cup of Water Illustration:

"Picture yourself lost in the desert, thirsty, and dehydrated to the point of death. Suddenly, a rescue team arrives and a man offers you a cup of cool water. Intellectually, you may believe in the power of water to quench your thirst and save your life. But, the water cannot save you until your parched lips *drink it.* You must choose to *receive it.* Believing without receiving is not enough. Spiritually, you must both *believe and receive* in order to become a child of God."

#4 Amplification: If He Is Not Ready To Receive Christ

If your Timothy reveals that he is *not sure* about having received Christ but wants to learn more about Him, be patient. Continue your meetings with the prayerful expectation that he will soon receive Christ. The material you cover in these next few sessions will help him clearly understand the gospel message.

If he does not decide to receive Christ and grow spiritually, pledge your prayer support, assure him of your continued interest, and report the situation to your Coordinator.

#5 Amplification: The Purpose Of *A Call To Joy*

Explain that receiving Jesus Christ as his personal Savior lays the *solid* foundation on which to build his life. That foundation is eternal. *"For no one can lay any foundation other than the one already laid, which is Jesus Christ."* (1 Corinthians 3:11, NIV) *A Call To Joy* is designed to give him the *practical tools and instruction* needed to build upon that foundation. The spiritual building blocks which God desires to use are more precious than gold, silver, or costly stones (1 Corinthians 3:11-15).

SESSION TWO

#6 Illustration: Marriage

Your Timothy may already be a church member, but still have remaining doubts about his salvation. This is usually the result of looking for a certain *feeling*, the presence of *unconfessed sin*, or the fact that he still has never *received* Christ.

Help him to understand that with Christ there is *no* middle ground (1 John 5:12). He cannot be partially or "sort of" a Christian. Marriage provides an excellent analogy. If you ask your Timothy if he is married, he will not say, "Well, I might be married." He will clearly know whether he is or not!

#7 Illustration: Young Man Who Runs Away From Home

Whenever a young man rebels and runs away from home, he remains the son of his parents no matter how far he runs, or how deeply he strays from his parent's values. He retains his *relationship* as a son in spite of the temporary loss of close *fellowship* with his parents. In the same way, it is possible to be God's child (a Christian) and temporarily rebel and be out of *fellowship* with Him. If this occurs, he will lose the "joy of his salvation," but not his relationship with God.

#8 Amplification: Assurance

Satan delights in tempting a Christian to think that he is not really a child of God, so brace your Timothy for this likelihood. Explain that *legitimate* guilt is brought to our attention by the Holy Spirit. This is produced by unconfessed sin in our lives. *Guilt feelings* which are *not legitimate* may come from low self-esteem or other psychological sources.

Explain that while feelings are important, they are also subject to change and are unreliable as a gauge for our relationship with Christ.

#9 Illustration: Ruth Graham

A person may not remember the exact date or hour of his conversion experience. Ruth Graham, the wife of the famous evangelist, became a Christian as a young child. Years later she summarized her testimony by saying, "I'm not sure *when* the sun came up, but I'm certain that it's shining!" It is *not* essential that a person remember the precise time of his conversion; but it is essential that he know for *certain* that he has personally received Christ as Savior.

#10 Illustration: Driving Around The Pumps

Imagine driving into a full-service gasoline station. As the attendant walks toward your car you say, "Fill 'er up please," but then you keep on driving around the pumps! The attendant looks perplexed as you continue to circle and call out the window, "Please fill 'er up!" Finally he starts chasing the car, trying to remove the gas cap. After much frustration, he removes the cap and points the gas nozzle in the general direction of your tank. What do you think will happen to most of the gas? You're right – it will be wasted. The point is easy to see. In your spiritual life, you must learn to be still in order to receive many of the blessings that God wants to give you!

SESSION 3

#11 Amplification: Informal Conversation

Pay special attention to anything your Timothy says or implies about relationships with his family, work associates, or friends.

Remember that the primary purpose of your time together is to minister to his individual and personal needs, not to complete a series of assignments. He will sense your attitude and deeply appreciate the fact that *his needs* are your foremost concern.

#12 Illustration: Leaky Bucket

Imagine a poor, thirsty farmer going to draw water from a well. Although the bucket is *full* when it leaves the bottom of the well, by the time it reaches the top it only contains a few drops of water. When this happens, its time for a decision. The farmer can either *fix* the leak in his bucket or resign himself to a life of being thirsty. Most Christians forget what they hear at church and lose the blessing of growth simply because they haven't tried to fix the leak!

#13 Illustration: A Good Athlete

A good track-man works out when he *feels* like it and he works out when he *doesn't* feel like it. He trains *daily*. Why? Because he knows that consistency can make the difference between winning and losing the race.

#14 Illustration: You Don't Quit Eating

If you miss a Quiet Time, don't become discouraged and stop having Quiet Times altogether. Let me illustrate this thought. What if you came to me and said,
"(Your name), I am so discouraged."
"I'm sorry to hear that, What's wrong?"
You respond, "I missed a meal yesterday and I made a commitment to become a serious 'eater.' I guess I just don't have what it takes to be faithful, so I'm going to give up eating altogether."
No one gives up eating just because they miss a meal or two. The Bible is our spiritual food and we don't give up our Quiet Times just because we miss one.
Your physical hunger reminds you to visit the refrigerator, and your spiritual hunger should remind you to enjoy your Bible. Self imposed starvation and malnutrition are spiritually foolish, so use good common sense and feed yourself. Many Christians eat only one spiritual meal per week – on Sunday. What kind of physical

condition would you be in if you only ate one meal each week?

#15 Illustration: The Redwood Trees

Have you ever seen a picture of the huge redwood trees in northern California? Most of them are hundreds of years old. These trees have endured every conceivable kind of weather condition, yet they continue to grow.

One would assume that such trees would also have deep massive root systems, but in fact they are shallow. Their roots are so inadequate that they could never stand on their own. The key to their tremendous strength is hidden beneath the surface, where their roots are intertwined. Over the years, each new tree has gained its support from all the others.

In the same way, your Timothy will gain strength and support from the fellowship and prayers of other committed Christian friends.

SESSION 4

#16 Illustration: "Billy Graham"

During one crusade in a foreign country, Billy Graham looked lovingly and compassionately toward those who had come forward to make decisions for Christ. He asked them, "Do you know how to pray?" Then he looked toward heaven and said, "Father, I love you." Looking back at the crowd, he quietly said, "That's how you pray."

SESSION 5

#17 Illustration: "Missionary in Africa"

A missionary in Africa once found himself in the path of a charging lion. After a frantic attempt to outrun the lion, he dropped to his knees in desperation crying "God – save me or I'll die!" A moment later, the huge animal leaped over him and ran away in pursuit of a gazelle. The breathless missionary was overwhelmed with gratitude, and thanked the Lord for this amazing deliverance!

That night, as he tried to sleep, a tiny mosquito began to bother him. Each time the exhausted minister started to doze, the pesky mosquito would begin buzzing in his ear. He swatted blindly in the darkness, but without success. Finally, he grabbed his flashlight and searched in vain for the mosquito. All through the night he tossed and turned without success.

The next morning, while having a rather drowsy Quiet Time, he read the passage in Philippians where Paul said, *"Pray about everything."* (4:6b, TLB) He sensed God saying, "Yesterday when you had a big need, you called on Me instantly, but last night when your problem was small, you chose to handle it alone."

Teach your Timothy to trust God with small needs as well as big ones. He cares about *every* aspect of your life, so never worry about "bothering" Him with something you consider to be small. If it concerns you, it concerns your heavenly Father as well.

SESSION 6

#18 Illustration: "Zipper"

This is kind of a silly illustration. I want you to pretend that I've got a big zipper on my back. We are out playing tennis together and I'm playing very badly. Then a top tennis pro walks up and says,

"Young man you seem to be having a difficult time."

"I sure am!" I reply.

He then says, "May I make a suggestion? The problem is, you need to understand the feel of the game. You just don't have the movement, freedom, or the motion that you need. I wish there was some way I could get inside you and let you experience the game of tennis the way I do. You're too stiff and mechanical."

Then I reply, "Well there is a way!" So we walk behind a big tree and I show him. "Look, I've got this big zipper on my back; just step in."

He says, "I have never seen anything like that before!" So he steps in. You know, it's very difficult to let somebody else live in you. So, I try to give him complete control. As he starts trying to walk around in my body, I can hear him saying, "Be loose, be limber, relax. Let me play the game *through* you." Next, He takes the tennis racket and *boom!*, it lands in the court for a change! And it lands with great power! As you look on, you are totally amazed and can't believe what you are seeing. Soon, they start bringing all the top tennis players to play against me, and I quickly beat them all. I think this is so easy because *he* is doing the work. If I start to stiffen up a little he says," Now just relax, let me play *through* you. Let *me* do the work."

And then I start to get a little pride in my heart. I say, "You know, I think I can do this myself now. I think I can serve better if I lift my left foot and make a little circle with it before I hit the ball."

He says, "If you do that, you'll land right on your face."

I reply, "Well, let me try it anyway." I try it and land right on my face.

He says, "Would you like me to take over again?"

"Yes, I did look pretty silly flat on my face. Please take over again."

Before we receive Christ as our Savior, we try to live life on our own without true peace, guidance, and fulfillment. After we receive Him, God gives us the Holy Spirit to be our power source for living a godly life.

The Holy Spirit does not want to be in our lives just as a passenger, He wants to empower and enable us to live a victorious Christian life! The more we yield to His control, the more He can work *through* us!

#19 Illustration: "Lawnmower"

A friend of mine, Charles Price, tells this true story:

On one of my frequent absences from home, the grass on our lawn needed cutting. We had recently purchased a new motor mower, which my wife Hilary had seen me use several times. Knowing I would not be back for several days, and that the fine weather was not likely to last until then, she decided to mow the grass. The mower was fairly solid, with rotary blades, a roller, and petrol motor weighing down on the machine. She started the engine, which automatically began to turn the blades in its stationary position, and then she began to push. It was really hard work! To get any movement took almost all her strength, but determined as she was, she applied all her might and with all her body against the mower at a forty-five degree angle, she gave it everything she had until after two lengths of the lawn she was exhausted!

This was very confusing. She had seen me walking up and down the lawn behind the mower, apparently effortlessly. Although she knew I was stronger than she was, she knew the difference wasn't as great as this! In frustration and anger she grabbed hold of the handle to give the machine a good shake and in so doing caught the clutch lever and engaged it. Suddenly the mower took off across the lawn under its own power, cutting the grass in its path with Hilary flying out behind it! What a marvellous difference!

How frustrating to find yourself manually operating something designed to run on its own power! And how wonderfully liberating to discover after a long, hard, tiring struggle that there are resources at your disposal you knew nothing about. This has been the personal experience of many people right through history. They have tried with the utmost sincerity and dedication to do for God what only God Himself could do for them. There was no fault in their zeal or failure in their enthusiasm. They just did not know or *appropriate* the indwelling presence of the Holy Spirit. God provides the Holy Spirit to help us accomplish His will.

#20 Illustration: "Sponge"

Imagine for a minute that you have a sponge in your hand. Squeeze the sponge tightly; now submerge it completely in a bucket of water. At this very moment, though the sponge is in the water, very little water is in the sponge. It is only when you release your grip that the sponge is filled.

In this same manner, your will can keep you from being filled and controlled by God's Spirit. This possibility constantly exists even though as a Christian you were baptized into His body by His Spirit when you were born again.

The key to being filled with the Holy Spirit is in remaining yielded and totally open to the will of God. Don't quench the working of God's Spirit by attempting to rule and possess your own life. Lordship means exactly what you might expect. Serving Christ best and enjoying life most comes when we continually yield to His perfect will. Spiritual power comes as a result of being filled, and being filled comes as a result of being controlled. Being controlled comes as a result of the moment-by-moment decision to be yielded.

SESSION 7

#21 Illustration: "Indian Chief"

In the folklore of the American Indians, a story is told about a brave who once asked an aging chief this question: "If two puppies are born to the same mother at the same time, which one will be the strongest?" The old chief wisely replied, "The one you feed the most!"

As a Christian, you can either feed your new nature and become spiritually strong, or you can choose to live in weakness and compromise. Through Christ, you are free to make right choices all day, every day! The Bible says, *"If the Son shall make you free, you shall be free indeed."* Mentally, we can feed on anything we choose, but our lives will reflect the quality of our choices.

#22 Illustration: "Black Ink"

If black ink were continually allowed to drip into a bucket of pure white paint, how long do you think it would take for the white paint to turn gray? Not very long. Eventually, it would become jet black! In the same way, each sinful thought endangers the purity of your mind. However, by meditating on the verses you memorize, you can restore and increase that purity.

#23 Illustration: "Charles Swindoll"

Charles Swindoll, a well-known North American pastor and author, tells about an incident which happened to him while ministering in a foreign country. Feeling a little bored and lonely, he walked toward his hotel elevator to go up to his room. En route, he passed two young women who followed him into the elevator. After pushing the button for the sixth floor, he politely asked, "What floor?" One of the women looked at him and said, "How about your floor?" In that moment, a thought flashed across his mind. Was it about his wife and four children? No, not at first. Was it about his position as a pastor and his reputation? No. God reminded him of two memory verses: *"Be not deceived; God is not mocked: for whatsoever a man soweth, that shall he also reap."* (Galatians 6:7, KJV); and *"Put on the full armor of God, that you may be able to stand firm against the schemes of the devil."* (Ephesians 6:11, NASB) The first verse reminded him of the *consequences* of sin, and the other verse *challenged* him to stand firm against the enemy. In God's strength he was able to reply, "I'm not interested!"

#24 Amplification: "Learn the Context"

Originally, the Bible was not divided into chapters and verses; each complete thought was contained in a paragraph. Today, these complete thoughts often encompass several verses. For that reason, when you memorize only one verse out of a complete thought, it is possible to miss the full meaning of the passage. Always teach your Timothy to read the verses immediately before and after his memory verse. Through this practice, he will gain a far better understanding of the verse he is planning to memorize.

APPENDIX B
DISCIPLESHIP
FLOW
CHART

B

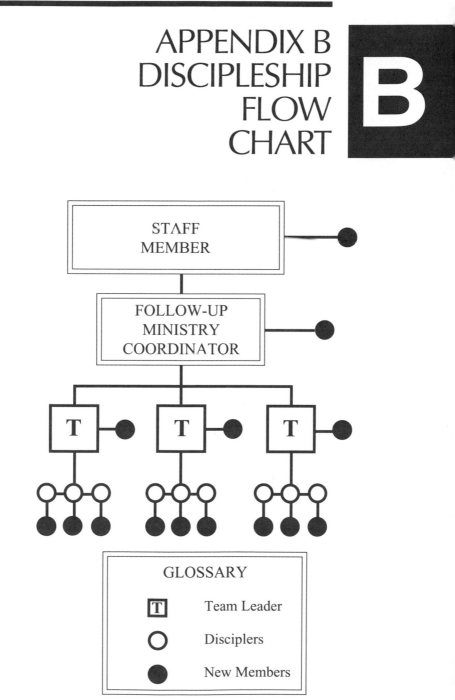

STAFF
MEMBER

FOLLOW-UP
MINISTRY
COORDINATOR

T   T   T

GLOSSARY

T	Team Leader
O	Disciplers
●	New Members

"If you love Me . . . feed My lambs." John 20:15

**No ministry deserves more
prayer, work, and consistency than
nurturing the new believers
in our flock.**

Your:

Coordinator's Name:

_____

Telephone Number: _____

Team Leader's Name:

_____

Telephone Number: _____

DISCIPLER'S FOLLOW-UP FORMS

❑ New Believer   ❑ New Member   Date: _____

New Friend's Name: _____
Street Address: _____
City: _____ Zip _____
Telephone: (Home) _____
                (Work) _____
Age: _____

❑ New Believer ❑ New Member Date: _____

New Friend's Name: _____
Street Address: _____
City: _____ Zip _____
Telephone: (Home) _____
(Work) _____
Age: _____

❑ New Believer ❑ New Member Date: _____

New Friend's Name: _____
Street Address: _____
City: _____ Zip _____
Telephone: (Home) _____
(Work) _____
Age: _____

❑ New Believer ❑ New Member Date: _____

New Friend's Name: _____
Street Address: _____
City: _____ Zip _____
Telephone: (Home) _____
(Work) _____
Age: _____

❑ New Believer ❑ New Member Date: _____

New Friend's Name: _____
Street Address: _____
City: _____ Zip _____
Telephone: (Home) _____
(Work) _____
Age: _____

❏ New Believer   ❏ New Member   Date: _____

New Friend's Name: _____

Street Address: _____

City: _____ Zip _____

Telephone: (Home) _____

              (Work) _____

Age: _____

❏ New Believer   ❏ New Member   Date: _____

New Friend's Name: _____

Street Address: _____

City: _____ Zip _____

Telephone: (Home) _____

              (Work) _____

Age: _____

❏ New Believer   ❏ New Member   Date: _____

New Friend's Name: _____

Street Address: _____

City: _____ Zip _____

Telephone: (Home) _____

              (Work) _____

Age: _____

❏ New Believer   ❏ New Member   Date: _____

New Friend's Name: _____

Street Address: _____

City: _____ Zip _____

Telephone: (Home) _____

              (Work) _____

Age: _____

❏ New Believer ❏ New Member Date: _____

New Friend's Name: _____
Street Address: _____
City: _____ Zip _____
Telephone: (Home) _____
           (Work) _____
Age: _____

❏ New Believer ❏ New Member Date: _____

New Friend's Name: _____
Street Address: _____
City: _____ Zip _____
Telephone: (Home) _____
           (Work) _____
Age: _____

❏ New Believer   Date: _____

New _____
Str _____ Address: _____
Ci _____ Zip _____
Telephone: (Home) _____
           (Work) _____
Age: _____

❏ New Believer ❏ New Member Date: _____

New Friend's Name: _____
Street Address: _____
City: _____ Zip _____
Telephone: (Home) _____
           (Work) _____
Age: _____